Presented To:

_____

From:

_____

Date:

_____

God's Little Devotional Book
for Graduates

Honor Books
Tulsa, Oklahoma

God's Little Devotional Book for Graduates

ISBN 1-56292-481-8

45-253-00264

Copyright © 2002 by Honor Books

P.O. Box 55388

Tulsa, Oklahoma 74155

God's Little Devotional Book
for Graduates

Introduction

Congratulations! You are graduating into a world poised to set the pace for a promising new millennium. Breathtaking technologies are drawing us closer to a global community. We are flooded with information, bombarded by choices, and staggered by moral dilemmas our parents and grandparents never imagined. It is a world filled to the brim with challenges and possibilities.

So how can you make good choices for your life in this bold, new world? How can you cut through the hype and find the answers you need to build a productive and fulfilling life for yourself?

In *God's Little Devotional Book for Graduates,* you will find the insight and wisdom needed to help you tame an imposing and uncharted frontier. The timeless truths presented in these pages will help you anchor your life on a solid foundation and give you the necessary edge to live a life filled with success and fulfillment.

> *The world wants your best,*
> *but God wants your all.*

For months Eric Liddell trained with his heart set on winning the 100-meter race at the Olympics of 1924. Many sportswriters predicted he would win. At the games, however, Liddell learned that the 100-meter race was scheduled to be run on a Sunday. This posed a major problem for him, because Liddell did not believe he could honor God by running on the Lord's Day. He bowed out of the race and his fans were stunned. Some who had praised him in the past now called him a fool. He came under intense pressure to change his mind, but Liddell stood firm.

Then a runner dropped out of the 400-meter race, which was scheduled on a weekday, and Liddell offered to fill the slot. This was not really "his race"—the distance was four times as long as the race for which he had trained diligently. Even so, Liddell crossed the tape as victor and set a record of 47.6 seconds in the process. He had earned an Olympic gold medal . . . and made an uncompromising stand for his faith.

Liddell went on to become a missionary in China, where he died in a war camp in 1945. He lives in history as a man known more for his inner mettle than for his gold medal.

Thou shalt love the Lord thy God with all thy heart, and with all thy soul, and with all thy mind.
MATTHEW 22:37

Warmiwañusca, aptly translated "Dead Woman's Pass," loomed in front of Debra like an impenetrable fortress. The pass rose 13,750 feet—seemingly straight up. Debra longed for a switchback, or better yet, a 7-11. Halfway up, she had her first bout with altitude sickness. But there was no way she'd turn back.

Her guide suggested she try the Peruvian "Walk of the Patient One." "Take one step only one inch ahead of your last," he explained. "Don't try to keep up with the others. Go at the pace God designed you for."

The best thing about the future is that it comes only one day at a time.

Debra not only reached the top but finished the four-day trek over Peru's Inca Trail. The forty-year-old mother of two fulfilled a dream she'd had since she was twelve. "If I'd known what the path was going to be like, I never would have gone," she said. "I would've thought I'd never make it. And I would have missed the greatest adventure of my life."

Graduation is a time of great expectations and adventures. In His wisdom, however, God only lets you see as far ahead as today. When life's rough mountain peaks and deep valleys stand in the way of your goals, don't be discouraged. Take your eyes off those around you. Take a fresh look at the person God designed you to be. Then continue toward your destination, one step at a time.

"Don't be anxious about tomorrow.
God will take care of your tomorrow too.
Live one day at a time."
MATTHEW 6:34 TLB

> *Shoot for the moon.*
> *Even if you miss it you*
> *will land among the stars.*

As Peter Bird approached Australia's Great Barrier Reef, he was courageous enough to do something he'd dreaded for the last 8,990 miles of his journey—call for help. Rowing alone across the Pacific Ocean from San Francisco to Australia was a valiant goal—one that had never before been achieved. Faced with turbulent waves from a raging storm, Bird radioed for help only thirty-three miles short of his final destination.

Bird made it to Australia, though not the way he'd originally planned. His boat, wasn't so lucky. As it was being towed to shore, it broke apart in the choppy seas. Bird had made a wise decision in asking for help. Obviously, he was disappointed at the outcome of his voyage, but did that make his attempt any less heroic?

The question: "What would you do if you knew you couldn't fail?" isn't really a fair one. Without the possibility of failure, there can be no real sense of victory or accomplishment. Without risk, there's no room for courage to grow. The real question is, "What would you attempt, even if you knew you might fail?" Aiming for perfection doesn't ensure you'll reach it. It merely keeps you headed in the right direction. Are the goals you've set in your life only those you know you can achieve, or are you willing to take a chance and grow?[1]

Aim for perfection.

2 CORINTHIANS 13:11 NIV

The difference between success and failure is often the ability to get up just one more time than you fall down! Consider the lives of these Bible characters:

- Moses easily could have given up. He had an "interrupted" childhood and lived with a foster family. He also had a strong temper, a stammering tongue, and a criminal record, but when God called him, he said "yes."

The man who wins may have been counted out several times, but he didn't hear the referee.

- Joshua had seen the Promised Land, but he was not allowed to enter. Instead, he was forced to wander in the wilderness for forty years with cowards who didn't believe, as he did, that they could conquer their enemies and possess the land. He could have given up in discouragement, but he held on to God's promises.

- Peter did not have a smooth transition from fisherman to apostle. He sank while trying to walk on water, was strongly rebuked by Jesus for trying to tell Him what to do, and denied knowing Jesus when Jesus needed him most. He easily could have seen himself as a hopeless failure; but when the opportunity came to preach the message of God's love before thousands on the Day of Pentecost, he was ready and willing

No matter what you've done, what mistakes you've made, what errors you may have committed, you're not a failure until you lay down and quit.

Though a righteous man falls
seven times, he rises again.
PROVERBS 24:16 NIV

15

*The secret of success is
to do the common things
uncommonly well.*

Helping the deaf to communicate was Alexander Graham Bell's motivation for his life's work, perhaps because his mother and wife were both deaf. "If I can make a deaf-mute talk," Bell said, "I can make metal talk." For five frustrating and impoverished years, he experimented with a variety of materials in an effort to make a metal disk that, vibrating in response to sound, could reproduce those sounds and send them over an electrified wire.

During a visit to Washington D.C., he called on Joseph Henry, a scientist who was a pioneer in research related to electricity. He presented his ideas to him and asked his advice: Should he let someone else perfect the telephone or should he do it himself? Henry encouraged him to do it himself, even though Bell complained that he lacked the necessary knowledge of electricity. Henry's brief solution was, "If you don't have it, get it."

So Bell studied electricity. A year later, while obtaining a patent for the telephone, the officials in the patent office credited him with knowing more about electricity than all the other inventors of his day combined.

Hard work. Study. Hope. Persistence. These are all "common things." They are also the keys to doing uncommonly well.

Seest thou a man diligent in his business?
he shall stand before kings;
he shall not stand before mean men.
PROVERBS 22:29

"Okay, God," prayed Becky. "This afternoon is set aside for you. I'm taking the next two hours just to pray." Becky had never talked to God that long before. Feeling that it might become difficult to stay with it, she wrote out an extensive list of people and problems she felt she needed to pray about.

Soon after she started, Becky felt that she should give her friend Teri a call. She'd wanted to invite Teri and her family over to lunch, but had never quite gotten around to asking them. Fearing that her mind was starting to wander, Becky tried to go back to her list, but Teri kept coming to mind. After several attempts to get her mind back on what she was doing, Becky gave up and phoned Teri.

Blessed is the man who finds out which way God is moving and then gets going in the same direction.

18

As Becky began to voice her invitation, Teri started laughing. Taken aback, Becky wondered what great social blunder she had just committed. Teri explained, "Just five minutes ago, I was having a regular pity party, crying because no one at our church ever invites us over. I had just said those very words to my husband when the phone rang."

Are you willing to let God change your agenda? His timing is always perfect. Today when you pray, be sure to listen for God's voice speaking to your heart even as you verbalize your concerns to Him. Why settle for a monologue when you can enjoy a two-way conversation.

Whether you turn to the right or to the left, your ears will hear a voice behind you, saying, "This is the way; walk in it."

ISAIAH 30:21 NIV

> *Never think that God's delays are*
> *God's denials. Hold on; hold fast;*
> *hold out. Patience is genius.*

Theodor was an artist, of sorts. He drew cartoons for a "creature-of-the-month" ad campaign for a popular insecticide called "Flit." Theodor, however, wanted to expand the scope of his commercial illustrating. Unfortunately, his advertising contract wouldn't allow it, forcing him to try his hand at writing and illustrating children's books.

After twenty-seven rejections of his first attempt, *A Story No One Can Beat,* Theodor was ready to give up. On his way home to burn his manuscript, Theodor ran into an old schoolmate who had just been hired as a children's book editor at Vanguard Press. With a change of the title to *And To Think It Began on Mulberry Street,* Theodor's first book finally made it to press.

Thus began the career of the best-selling children's author of all time, Theodor Seuss Geisel. In addition to winning the Pulitzer Prize for fiction in 1984, "Dr. Seuss" was also awarded eight honorary degrees. When he died at the age of eighty-seven, Theodor's books had sold more than 200 million copies, and he was receiving nearly 1,500 fan letters a week.[2]

How soon is too soon to give up? It is any time before you're absolutely certain God wants you to head in a new direction. After all, who knows what unexpected rewards the second try, the tenth, or the twenty-seventh will hold?

Whenever you face trials of any kind, consider it nothing but joy, because you know that the testing of your faith produces endurance.

JAMES 1:2-3 NRSV

Charles Oakley, forward for the New York Knicks and an NBA All-star, has a reputation for being one of basketball's best rebounders. It's his toughness, however, that has probably contributed the most to his outstanding sports career.

While other professional players seem to have frequent injuries or are sidelined for other reasons, Oakley has had very few injuries over the course of his thirteen-year career, even though he has absorbed a great deal of physical punishment on the court. He is often pushed and fouled. He puts in miles each game,

No horse gets anywhere until he is harnessed. No life ever grows great until it is focused, dedicated, disciplined.

running up and down the court. He frequently dives into the stands for loose balls, to the extent that the courtside media teases him about being a working hazard. According to

Oakley, his tenacity and energy were instilled in him by his grandfather, Julius Moss.

Moss was a farmer in Alabama who did most of his field work by hand. "Other people had more equipment than he did," Oakley says. "He didn't have a tractor, but he got the work done. No excuses." Moss, who died in 1990, developed all sorts of aches and pains in his life, but he laughed at them and went about his business. Oakley saw a lesson in that—nothing should prevent him from earning a day's pay.

Being focused, dedicated, and disciplined will make the difference between a mediocre life and a *great* life.

In a race, everyone runs but only one person gets first prize. . . . To win the contest you must deny yourselves many things that would keep you from doing your best.

1 CORINTHIANS 9:24-25 TLB

> *Nothing great was ever*
> *achieved without enthusiasm.*

After years of working in Rome on life-sized sculptures, Michelangelo went to Florence, where a large block of splendid white Carrara marble had been obtained for a colossal statue. Within weeks, he had signed an agreement to complete a rendition of David for the cathedral.

Contract in hand, he started in at once, working with a furious energy so great that he often slept in his clothes, resenting the time it took to take them off and put them on again. He faultlessly examined and precisely measured the marble to see what pose it could accommodate. He made sketches of possible attitudes and careful, detailed drawings from models. He tested his ideas in wax on a small scale. When he was finally satisfied with his design, only then did he pick up a chisel and mallet.

Michelangelo approached painting the ceiling of the Sistine Chapel with the same intensity. Lying at uncomfortable angles on hard boards, while breathing the suffocating air just under the vault, Michelangelo suffered with inflamed eyes and irritated skin from the plaster dust. For the next four years, he was literally sweating in physical distress as he worked.

If you aren't passionate about the work you do, find something about which you can become enthused. You may not be in a position to change jobs, but you can always find a hobby, develop a talent, or hone a skill. Such pursuits can greatly increase the joy of living.

The joy of the LORD is your strength.
NEHEMIAH 8:10

A story is told about the chance meeting of Pablo Picasso and an American soldier. The two of them were seated at a Parisian café and decided to share a drink or two. It wasn't surprising that their conversation soon turned to art. So Picasso tried to explain to the soldier the style of art for which he was known.

"I just don't like modern art," remarked the soldier.

When Picasso asked him why not, the soldier said that modern art was not realistic. He said that he preferred paintings that actually looked like the things they were supposed to be paintings of.

Picasso said nothing. To break the uncomfortable silence, the soldier decided to

The world is governed more by appearances than realities.

share a few photos from his wallet of his girlfriend back in the States. Picasso looked at each of the photos politely. Then holding one of the photos in his hand, he commented to the soldier, "Goodness! Is she really this small?"[3]

Every situation in your life can be seen from a variety of angles, each presenting a different point of view. There is, however, only one true reality—life seen from God's point of view. There is a bigger picture, an eternal one, hidden behind the canvas of every ordinary day. Even though you can't always see it, it is there.

These are a shadow of the things
that were to come; the reality,
however, is found in Christ.
COLOSSIANS 2:17 NIV

Do all the good you can to all the people you can, in all the ways you can, as often as ever you can, as long as you can.

The restaurant was almost empty. Still, the waiter seated Lisa and her grandmother right next to a single businessman, who was enjoying his newspaper and a leisurely lunch. Lisa began to panic. She was accustomed to her grandmother's idiosyncrasies since the onset of Alzheimer's, but she wasn't sure the businessman would be as understanding.

As soon as they were seated, the questions began. "How am I going to pay for this food? I don't have any money. Who's paying my bills? I shouldn't have moved here. I'm just a burden. Why don't you leave me in the gutter to die?"

Patiently, Lisa tried to calm her grandmother's fears, answering the same questions she answered week after week. Forty minutes passed. Lisa couldn't stop worrying about the man sitting next to them. *He's trying to relax,* she thought. *My grandmother's probably driving him crazy.*

Lisa was relieved when the man finally folded his paper and prepared to leave. Then to her surprise, he headed straight for their table. Lisa prepared to apologize for any aggravation her grandmother might have caused him. Instead, he looked at Lisa with a smile and whispered, "When I get older, I hope I have a granddaughter just like you."

Even the smallest gesture of kindness can make a big difference in someone's life. Keep your eyes and heart open for the opportunities today brings.

Do not forget to do good and to share with others, for with such sacrifices God is pleased.

HEBREWS 13:16 NIV

None of the kids on the block knew why Mrs. Greer was so mean. All they knew for sure was that she hated kids. If a ball rolled into her yard, they forgot it. After knocking on her door once, no one ever tried it again. One day, out of spite, the elderly woman turned on her sprinkler. Instead of watering her front lawn, it was set to water the sidewalk, preventing the children from even riding their bikes in front of her house.

If you can't change your circumstances, change the way you respond to them.

Not being old enough to cross the street on their own, one of their favorite pastimes came to a standstill. Then a smile spread across one child's face, and as he whispered his idea to the others, smiles spread throughout the group. Each kid ran home with a mission. On that sunny, cloudless day the children returned with their bikes—and their raincoats. Their bike ride became a wet and wild adventure, as they rode through the sprinklers, laughing harder than they had with their original game.

When you are faced with difficult circumstances, the decision is yours. You can let a seed of bitterness rob you of joy, like it did the old woman; or you can let circumstances stretch your creativity and lead you in a new direction. Who knows, you may find yourself somewhere you never expected, grateful for the new opportunity.

We know that in all things God works for the good of those who love him, who have been called according to his purpose.

ROMANS 8:28 NIV

*Things are not always
what they seem.*

Donna and Gillian had planned their trip to Hawaii for more than a year. All the planning in the world, however, could not have prepared them for the unexpected death of one of their dearest friends right before they were to leave. In silence, they boarded the plane. They were going to miss the funeral, but the tickets couldn't be changed. They had to go now—or never.

After the first leg of their trip, the plane was delayed. When their early afternoon connection finally departed after midnight, Donna expressed her frustration and anger. "We could have stayed for the funeral and still caught this stupid plane!" she muttered. Though a week on the beach lifted their spirits,

Donna and Gillian's bitterness over the late flight remained.

Then shortly after arriving at the airport for their return trip, they were startled by a woman's cry, "My baby's stopped breathing!" No one moved—except Donna. As a nurse, she knew exactly what to do. She gave the baby CPR and helped calm the mother until the ambulance arrived. It wasn't until they were on the plane that Gillian and Donna realized a startling fact. If they had made the earlier flight the week before, they would have picked up their rental car earlier and surrendered it earlier on the day they left. They would not have been there for the baby and his mother.

Even when circumstances seem meaningless or contrary, God has a plan. What a privilege to see your part in it.

The LORD does not look at the things man looks at. Man looks at the outward appearance, but the LORD looks at the heart.

1 SAMUEL 16:7 NIV

Driving a car pool to the zoo was one thing. Waiting in the parking lot for two hours for the drive home was quite another. Carol tried to read but decided a leisurely drive might relieve some of the anxiety she had been feeling lately. As she pulled out of the parking lot, a crack of thunder heralded an afternoon thunderstorm.

Down the road, a man and two young children stood shivering in the sudden rain. He held his thumb out tentatively. Carol never picked up hitchhikers, but she couldn't ignore someone who obviously needed help.

Blessed are those who see the hand of God in the haphazard, inexplicable, and seemingly senseless circumstances of life.

"My car broke down in the zoo parking lot," the stranger explained. "Could you please get me to a phone? I need to call someone who's waiting for us at Sammy's Café." Having time to kill, Carol insisted on driving them to the nearby restaurant.

During the drive, the man talked about the many tragedies he had suffered in his life and how God had worked through them. When they reached their destination, the man commented, "God works miracles through painful situations. You are so special to Him. He's going to bless you!"

As Carol drove back to the zoo, she couldn't help wondering. *Why hadn't the man used a phone at the zoo rather than hitchhiking?* Perhaps, because she needed to hear God's voice in a personal way that day. That was blessing enough.

I am with you and will watch
over you wherever you go.

GENESIS 28:15 NIV

> *There can be no such thing as a
> necessary evil. For if a thing is really
> necessary, it cannot be an evil and
> if it is an evil, it is not necessary.*

In the seventeenth century, Edinburgh was bustling with both aristocracy and peasants, all living in very close quarters. The Scottish city was built on a hilltop with many enclosed stairways leading down to the city gates below. Each stairway, or "close," was shared by numerous families whose front doors opened onto it. Each close had a gate at the top and one at the bottom that were locked at night for protection. But the plague still found its way inside.

As word reached Edinburgh that the plague was spreading through the low-lying country-side, the city gates were locked to all outsiders. Soon, however, there was a small outbreak inside the city, in Mary King's Close. To prevent further spread of the disease, the city fathers decided upon a simple, yet heartless plan.

The gates to Mary King's Close were locked with all 400 residents inside. They were given no food or water and their cries of suffering were ignored, until finally there was only silence. Mary King's Close is locked to this day, a memorial to those whose deaths served as an easy solution.

When faced with a difficult decision, take time to make sure your solution is the best one, not simply the most expedient.

This is what the LORD says: "Stand at the crossroads and look; ask for the ancient paths, ask where the good way is, and walk in it, and you will find rest for your souls."
JEREMIAH 6:16 NIV

Arturo Toscanini was one of the greatest orchestral conductors of all time. Nicknamed "Genius" by his classmates at the Parma Conservatory where he studied cello for nine years, he also received the nickname "Scissors" for his sharp sense of criticism. After years of work in Europe, Toscanini was offered the chance to direct the newly formed NBC Symphony.

Many receive advice; only the wise profit by it.

Before he arrived in New York, Toscanini listened to the orchestra perform on a shortwave radio from his home in Milan, Italy. Endowed with perfect pitch, Toscanini could tell from all the way across the Atlantic that the first clarinetist was not on par with the rest of the orchestra. While "Scissors" could have easily criticized the musician and auditioned for a replacement, Toscanini instead offered advice. After working closely with Toscanini, the musician became one of the world's greatest clarinetists and stayed with the NBC Symphony for seventeen years.[4]

The difference between mediocrity and excellence can sometimes be bridged by acting on the advice of others. Everyone has different strengths and weaknesses. While comparison seems only natural, comparing one person's gifts to another is like comparing apples and oranges. They are simply created differently. Sharing wisdom from your areas of strength, and listening to others share theirs with you, provide a chance for growth. Is there someone's advice you could use right now?

Pride only breeds quarrels, but wisdom is found in those who take advice.

PROVERBS 13:10 NIV

> *The only way to have*
> *a friend is to be one.*

Mary Lennox "was not an affectionate child and had never cared much for anyone," and that was not so difficult to understand. Ignored by her parents and raised by servants, she had no concept of what life was like outside of India. Other children called her "Mistress Mary Quite Contrary," because she didn't like to share and always insisted on having her own way.

When Mary was nine years old, her parents died of cholera, and she was sent to live at her uncle's home in England. The move did nothing to improve her disposition. She expected anyone and everyone to jump when she snapped her fingers.

Gradually, however, Mary began to change. Realizing how lonely she was, she asked a robin in the garden to be her friend. She began treating her maid with more respect. Won over by the guilelessness of her maid's little brother, Dickon, and craving his approval, Mary found herself seeking his advice. She even revealed to him the location of her secret garden. Eventually, Mary convinced her crippled cousin, Colin, to grab hold of life with both hands. By the last page of *The Secret Garden*, Mary's transformation is complete. She is happy with herself and surrounded by friends.

To make a friend, you first must make a decision to be a friend.

A man that hath friends
must shew himself friendly.
PROVERBS 18:24

A small dog was struck by a car and tossed onto the shoulder of the road. A doctor, who just happened to be driving by, noticed that the dog was still alive, stopped his car, picked it up, and took it home with him. When the doctor had an opportunity to examine the dog closely, he found that it had suffered only minor cuts and abrasions. He cleaned its wounds and carried it to the garage, where he intended to provide a temporary bed.

A Christian must keep the faith, but not to himself.

The dog, however, wriggled free from his arms, jumped to the ground, and scampered off. "What an ungrateful dog," the doctor said to himself. He was glad that the dog had recovered so quickly but a little miffed that it had shown so little appreciation for his expert care.

The doctor thought no more about the incident until the next evening, when he heard a scratching at his front door. He opened the door to find that the little dog had returned with another injured dog at its side!

Be encouraged! You may never see the difference you make in someone's life or the difference that person will make in the lives of others, but those with whom you share God's love will *never* be the same.

Go ye into all the world, and
preach the gospel to every creature.
MARK 16:15

You may laugh out loud in the future at something you're eating your heart out over today.

Trevor knew he was supposed to sit quietly in church and pay attention, but the gurgling and rumbling in his stomach had captured his full attention. He tried holding his breath, closing his eyes, and even humming quietly to himself, but suddenly, what he feared most seemed inevitable. Noticing the panicked look on his face, his mother whispered, "Trevor, what's the matter?"

Trevor quickly whispered back, "I think I'm gonna be sick!" His mother told him that the restroom was at the back of the church. With that, Trevor darted up from the pew. He returned so quickly that his mother was a little worried. "Trevor, did you make it to the bathroom?"

Trevor replied with a smile, "I didn't have to mom. In the back of the church, they had a nice little box right by the door that says, 'For the Sick.'"[5]

What did you worry about when you were a kid? Monsters under your bed? Being the shortest kid in the class? The tallest? Never being able to master a two-wheeler? As we grow older, childhood fears seem almost ridiculously small; but as a child, they seemed monumental.

Let hindsight teach you something about the problems that may be overwhelming you today. A molehill right in front of you can loom larger than the mountain on the horizon, merely because of where you're standing.

Our light affliction, which is but for a moment, worketh for us a far more exceeding and eternal weight of glory.

2 CORINTHIANS 4:17

Beth focused her camera on the field of wildflowers. From a distance, it looked like a uniform blanket of purple. Closer inspection revealed individual flowers, similar in composition, yet each bearing a unique combination of leaves and petals. She finished the roll of film and called it a day.

It wasn't until she enlarged the wildflower photos, though, that she noticed it. Within each of the tiny purple flowers, which themselves were no larger than the eraser of a pencil, there was a ring of white. The enlargements revealed that the ring itself was made of a tiny circle of perfectly formed white flowers, each no bigger than the size of a pencil point. Without magnification, the intricate beauty these common wildflowers contained would have gone unnoticed.

The more we learn about the wonders of our universe, the more clearly we are going to perceive the hand of God.

God weaves hidden beauty into places too small to be seen by the human eye—distant planets, blood cells, DNA strands. Why the extravagance? Why go to the extra work, even if you are the Creator of the universe?

During the Renaissance period, artists carefully finished the backs of statues fashioned for churches. They did this even though they knew only the eyes of God would ever enjoy them. In the same way, God must take delight in the act of creation, as well as its outcome. As God's most precious creation, He takes delight in every detail that makes you who you are.

By faith we understand that the universe was formed at God's command, so that what is seen was not made out of what was visible.

HEBREWS 11:3 NIV

*The test of courage comes when we are
in the minority; the test of tolerance
when we are in the majority.*

Raoul Wallenberg was a Swedish diplomat in the 1940s. Though the Holocaust of World War II threatened many lives, Wallenberg's wasn't one of them. His work for the Swedish government put him in a safe and privileged position. Yet Wallenberg worked to help save the lives of Hungarian Jews.

Having business connections in Hungary, Wallenberg set up an office issuing fake passports. But he didn't stop there. He set up safe housing, soup kitchens, and hospitals for those he was extending bogus passports to. On one occasion, he saw Jews being loaded onto a train destined for the death camps. He demanded that all of the prisoners with passports get off the train. Prisoner's waved any piece of paper they could find at him—eyeglass prescriptions, driver's licenses, even deportation papers. He honored them all as passports, saving three hundred lives. It is estimated that during the war, Wallenberg offered diplomatic protection to approximately two hundred thousand Hungarian Jews—just because he felt it was the right thing to do.[6]

God chooses unlikely heroes. Take David, facing Goliath with nothing but a handful of stones; or Moses, raised in the privileged safety of Pharaohs house, yet leading the Israelites, simply because God asked him to. Doing the right thing, even when it doesn't seem very dramatic or noteworthy, takes courage. Has God hidden a hero inside of you?

Be on your guard; stand firm in the faith; be men of courage; be strong. Do everything in love.

1 CORINTHIANS 16:13-14 NIV

What does the list of books and authors below have in common?

- *Tarzan*, by Edgar Rice Burroughs.

- *Alice's Adventures in Wonderland*, by Lewis Carroll.

- *The Divine Comedy,* by Dante.

- *Grimm's Fairy Tales,* by the Brothers Grimm.

- *The Merchant of Venice,* by William Shakespeare.

- Works by Francis Bacon, Miguel de Cervantes, Socrates, John Calvin, Martin Luther, and Homer.

- The American Heritage Dictionary.

- Mother Goose.

- The Bible.

> *The mind grows by what it feeds on.*

The answer is that at some time in history, each of these books and authors was banned. Those who chose to read their words, if they could even obtain a copy in the first place, did so at their own risk. Today things have changed, at least in the United States. Here, individuals decide for themselves what they will read, watch, listen to, stand up for, and stand against.

Yet that parental admonition still rings true: With greater freedom, comes greater responsibility. What weighs heaviest when you form an opinion or make a decision? Your gut reaction? The general consensus? The way you were raised? How do you respond when someone's opinion differs from your own? Do you jump on your soapbox? Feel threatened? Or do you listen with love? Giving careful consideration to what you believe, and why, gives you the strength you need to stand in support of the crowd or alone against it.[7]

The mind controlled by the
Spirit is life and peace.

ROMANS 8:6 NIV

> *The greater part of our happiness*
> *depends on our disposition*
> *and not our circumstances.*

Kara pressed her face against the window of her train compartment. Even though the sun had set long ago, she didn't want to miss a thing. It was her first trip to Egypt, and everything seemed so different from her home in California. That morning, an exodus of angry cockroaches had greeted her when she turned on the hotel shower, and one quick surge from her blowdryer was enough to blackout the power on the entire floor. Egypt didn't feel like another country. It felt like another world.

After miles of dimly lit desert, her eyes were drawn to a flicker of light. As the train approached, she saw it was a fire, surrounded by tents. A group of men were nearby, laughing animatedly. A young boy was reading a book by firelight, a camel enjoying the blaze by his side. Kara immediately felt sorry for the boy. *Probably a student like me,* she thought. Only here he was trying to do his homework by firelight and sleeping in a makeshift tent. Something about the boy's expression made her reconsider. Who was she to argue with such a contented smile?

Circumstances change daily. If your happiness depends solely on what's going on around you, it cannot last. If your joy comes from what is going on inside you, however, you can carry it with you wherever you go.

I know how to live on almost nothing or with everything. I have learned the secret of contentment in every situation.

PHILIPPIANS 4:12 TLB

Trina and Heather carefully placed their beach chairs by the edge of the water—close enough to get their feet wet, but not so close that a wave would splash salt water on their books. By the third day of their family vacation, the sisters had it down to an exact science—or so they thought.

One moment, Heather was seated next to Trina, reading. The next, Trina looked over and Heather was gone. Rolled up in her beach chair, Heather was tumbling end over end toward the ocean as the rogue wave receded. After the salt water was coughed up, the mountain of sand dislodged from her suit, and the convulsive laughter calmed to a controlled giggle, Heather turned to Trina and said, "You didn't even get wet! No fair!"

> *To believe in God is to know that the rules will be fair—and that there will be many surprises!*

Sometimes life just doesn't look fair. One person sits relaxing on the beach while another faces a mini-tidal wave trauma. One person wins the lottery while another faces financial ruin. One person's medical test results come back negative, another's positive.

God is always with you in the face of every surprise, both welcome and unwelcome. It is your heart, and not your circumstances, that will determine whether each "surprise" will draw you away from Him, or even closer to His side.

"I am the Way—yes, and the Truth and the Life."
JOHN 14:6 TLB

*I have never been hurt
by anything I didn't say.*

A young attorney, just out of law school and beginning his first day on the job, sat down in the comfort of his brand-new office with a great sigh of satisfaction. He had worked long and hard for the opportunity to savor such a moment. Then, noticing a prospective client coming toward his door, he tried to look busy and energetic.

Opening his legal pad and uncapping his pen, he picked up the telephone, and cradling it under his chin, began to write furiously. "Look, Harry, about that amalgamation deal," he said to an empty phone line. "I think I better run down to the factory and handle it personally. Yes. No. I don't think three million dollars will swing it. We should have Smith from LA meet us there. Okay. Get back to me."

Hanging up the phone, he put down his pen, looked up at his visitor, stood, extended his hand, and said in his most polite but confident attorney's voice, "Good morning. How might I help you?" The prospective client replied, "Actually, I'm just here to hook up your phone."

There's an old saying that goes, "A shut mouth gathers no foot." Sometimes the best thing to do is just keep your mouth shut!

Don't talk so much. You keep putting your foot in your mouth. Be sensible and turn off the flow!

Proverbs 10:19 TLB

One day, a boy at summer camp received a box of cookies from his mother. He ate a few, then placed the box under his bed. The next day, he discovered the cookies were gone. Later, a counselor who had been told of the theft saw a boy sitting behind a tree eating the stolen cookies. He sought out the victim and said, "Bill, I know who stole your cookies. Will you help me teach him a lesson?" The boy replied, "Well, I guess—but aren't you going to punish him?"

We too often love things and use people, when we should be using things and loving people.

The counselor said, "Not directly—that would only make him hate you. I have an idea, but first I want you to ask your mother to send some more cookies." The boy did as the counselor asked, and a few days later, another box of cookies arrived.

The counselor then said, "The boy who stole your cookies is by the lake. I suggest you go down there and share your cookies with him." The boy protested, "But he's the one who stole the first ones from me!" "I know," said the counselor. "Let's see what happens."

An hour later, the counselor saw the boys coming up the hill together. The thief was earnestly trying to get his new friend to accept his compass in payment for the stolen cookies, while the victim just as adamantly refused, saying a few old cookies didn't matter all that much!

Often the best way to "get back at someone" is to show them God's love. You can usually make a friend in the process.

Be devoted to one another in brotherly love.
Honor one another above yourselves.
ROMANS 12:10 NIV

*When you flee temptation,
don't leave a forwarding address.*

Velazquez Polk and Janet Kuzmaak both grew up in Portland, Oregon, but their lives could not have been more different. Polk was a tough street kid who joined a gang at age ten and was eventually arrested for selling drugs. Kuzmaak was an honor student from an upper-class neighborhood.

In 1980, Kuzmaak's sister was raped and murdered. Because authorities never solved the crime, she came to regard every criminal as her sister's killer.

Eventually, Kuzmaak became a nurse at a major medical center, and Polk, released from jail in 1990, was given a job as her surgical aide.

Kuzmaak was furious. She didn't believe in rehabilitation for criminals, but she noticed that when Polk's gang-member friends tried to entice him to rejoin their ranks, he refused. He told her that he wanted to flee his old life and join a program to become a nurse's aide. She remembered that her sister had once befriended a man on parole, so she lobbied the hospital to pay Polk's tuition while she continued to monitor him.

Today, Kuzmaak and Polk are great friends. She helped him gain entrance into a world he barely knew existed. And he helped her sweep away the bitterness that had once poisoned her heart.

Change and growth are always possible if you turn from evil and refuse to look back.

Now flee from youthful lusts, and pursue after righteousness . . . with those who call on the Lord from a pure heart.
2 TIMOTHY 2:22 NASB

As each new workday began, Harv looked out his storefront window and grumbled about his competitor's windows across the street. "They have the dirtiest windows in town," he'd tell customers. "They don't take a bit of pride in their establishment's appearance!"

One day, a customer suggested that Harv get his own windows cleaned. Harv took his advice. Low and behold, the next morning when Harv looked out the window he was amazed. "I can't believe it!" he commented to his head clerk. "As soon as I washed my windows, that lazy store manager across the street must have cleaned his, as well!"

Whatever you dislike in another person, take care to correct in yourself.

It's easy to criticize others—especially behind their backs. Criticism, however, is only "constructive" when it's said face-to-face and is motivated solely by concern for someone you love. When was the last time your words measured up to those high standards?

What you criticize in someone else reveals more about your own heart than it does another person's flaws. When are you most prone to criticize others? When you're feeling threatened or inferior? When jealousy or pride takes over? When you want to impress others or make them laugh? The next time critical words spring to mind, take a moment to be critical about your own life. Will what you're about to say have a positive or negative influence on those who hear it?

"Why do you look at the speck of sawdust in your brother's eye and pay no attention to the plank in your own eye?"

MATTHEW 7:3 NIV

Definition of status: Buying something you don't need with money you don't have to impress people you don't like.

Guy de Maupassant's *The Necklace* is the story of a young woman, Mathilde, who desires desperately to be accepted into high society. One day her husband, an ordinary man, is given an invitation to an elegant ball. Mathilde borrows a necklace from a wealthy friend to wear to the occasion and receives many compliments from the aristocracy present during the evening. Sadly, she discovers later that night that she has lost the necklace.

Mathilde's husband borrows 36,000 francs in an effort to replace the lost jewelry. He is forced to tap every resource available to him. Finally, a look-alike necklace is created, and Mathilde gives it to her friend, without telling her what had happened.

For ten years, the couple slaves to pay back the borrowed francs, each of them working two jobs. They are forced to sell their home and live in a slum. One day after the debt had finally been paid, Mathilde runs into her well-to-do friend and confesses that the necklace she returned was not the one she borrowed. To her consternation, she learns that the necklace loaned to her had been made from fake gemstones! The borrowed necklace had been worth less than 500 francs.

Trying to keep up appearances almost always leads to falling flat on your face.

"They do all their deeds to be noticed by men."
MATTHEW 23:5 NASB

To the casual observer, it seemed Basilio Clark couldn't do anything right. He couldn't even kill himself properly. He and eight of his fellow gang members had been arrested for murder and robbery in their homeland of the Philippines. After being sentenced to the electric chair, Basilio and his friends combined insecticide and paint thinner. They drank the deadly mixture as a group. Though rendered blind by the poison, Basilio was the only one who survived.

I like the dreams of the future better than the history of the past.

Recuperating in his cell, Basilio began listening to a radio that a woman who worked with the prisoners had given him. The radio received only one station, the Far East Broadcasting Company. As Basilio listened day after day, he learned about a God who loved him and forgave everything he'd done in the past. As Basilio's heart began to change on the inside, others began to notice a change on the outside as well. This was no longer the same angry young man who had terrorized the town of Olongapo. Eventually, the president of the Philippines issued a pardon for Basilio. Once released from prison, Basilio became a pastor, reaching out to others in love, instead of hate.[8]

Where you've come from doesn't have to determine where you're going. Is there anything in your past you'd like to change? God can help you. He's the author of fresh, new starts.

*Remember ye not the former things,
neither consider the things of old.
Behold, I will do a new thing.*
ISAIAH 43:18-19

*The way to get to the top
is to get off your bottom.*

One day, in the fall of 1894, Guglielmo retreated to his room on the third floor of his parents' home. He had just spent his entire summer vacation reading books and filling notebooks with squiggly diagrams. Now the time had come to work.

He rose early every morning. He worked all day and long into the night, to the point that his mother became alarmed. He had never been a robust person, but now he was appallingly thin. His face was drawn, and his eyes were often glazed over with fatigue.

Finally, the day came when he announced his instruments were ready. He invited the family to his room, and pushing a button, he succeeded in ringing a bell on the first floor!

While his mother was amazed, his father was not. He saw no use in being able to send a signal so short a distance. So Guglielmo labored on. Little by little, he made changes in his invention so he could send a signal from one hill to the next, and then beyond the hill. Eventually, his invention was perfected, partly by inspiration, but mostly by perseverance.

Guglielmo Marconi eventually was hailed as the inventor of wireless telegraphy—the forerunner of the radio. He not only received a Nobel prize in physics for his efforts, but also a seat in the Italian senate and many honorary degrees and titles.

You can accomplish anything you set your heart on by combining your vision with hard work.

How long will you lie down, O sluggard?
When will you arise from your sleep?
PROVERBS 6:9 NASB

Joe Smith was a loyal carpenter who worked almost two decades for a successful contractor. The contractor called him into his office one day and said, "Joe, I'm putting you in charge of the next house we build. I want you to order all the materials and oversee the job from the ground up."

Joe accepted the assignment with great enthusiasm. He studied the blueprints and checked every measurement and specification. Suddenly, he had a thought. *If I'm really in charge, why couldn't I cut a few corners, use less expensive materials, and put the extra money in my pocket? Who will know? Once the house is painted, it will look great.*

So Joe set about his scheme. He ordered second-grade lumber and inexpensive

> *You are only what you are when no one is looking.*

concrete, put in cheap wiring, and cut every corner he could. When the home was finished, the contractor came to see it.

"What a fine job you've done!" he said. "You've been such a faithful carpenter to me all these years that I've decided to show you my gratitude by giving you a gift—this house."

Build well today. You will have to live with the character and reputation you construct.

Not with eye-service, as men-pleasers;
but as the servants of Christ,
doing the will of God from the heart.
EPHESIANS 6:6

> *Take time to deliberate; but when the time for action arrives, stop thinking and go on.*

As long as he could remember, Jason had wanted to be a police officer. It wasn't just the fact that he loved playing cops and robbers. Jason wanted to do something that mattered with his life.

After graduation, Jason had the chance to apply for a spot at the police academy, but first came the interview. When the veteran officer pulled up a chair in front of him, Jason realized his childhood dream could rest upon this very moment. As he confidently answered each question, he felt the officer's approval. Jason knew he was doing well.

"One last question," the officer said. "Suppose you're called to help at the site of an explosion. There are numerous casualties.

Nearby, you notice a woman has gone into labor. At the same time, you see a car, whose driver is obviously intoxicated, weaving down the road toward an elementary school. Then, you hear a cry from someone drowning in a nearby river, while a fight erupts next to you that could result in both injury and property damage. What do you do?"

Jason thought a moment, then replied, "Try and hide my uniform and mingle with the crowd?"

Some situations in life take more than just a cool head, they take a miracle. Prayer without the courage to act upon what you hear is useless.

Rise up; this matter is in your hands. We will support you, so take courage and do it.
EZRA 10:4 NIV

According to an old fable, three men once decided to engage in the religious practice of absolute silence. They mutually agreed to keep a "day of quiet" from dawn until the stroke of midnight, at which time a full moon was expected to rise from the horizon. They sat cross-legged for hours, concentrating on the distant horizon, eager for darkness to envelop them.

One of them unwittingly noted, "It's difficult not to say anything at all."

The second one replied, "Quiet. You're speaking during the time of silence!"

There are times when silence is golden, other times it is just plain yellow.

The third man sighed and then boasted, "Now I'm the only one who hasn't spoken yet."

A rap singer has updated some of the advice given in the book of Ecclesiastes:

- There's a time to speak up and a time to shut up.

- There's a time to hunker down and a time to go downtown.

- There's a time to talk and a time to walk.

- There's a time to be mellow and a time not to be yellow.

Silence can be good, but never if it's the result of raw fear or lack of moral fiber.

*To everything there is a season . . . a time
to keep silence, and a time to speak.*

ECCLESIASTES 3:1-7

Every job is a self-portrait of the person who does it. Autograph your work with excellence.

A band of minstrels from a faraway land traveled about singing and playing their music in hopes of making a living, but they had not been doing well. Times were hard, and the common people had little money to spend on concerts, even though their fee was small.

The group met one evening to discuss their plight. "I see no reason for opening tonight," one said. "It's snowing, and no one will come out on a night like this." Another said, "I agree. Last night we performed for just a handful. Even fewer will come tonight."

The leader of the troupe responded, "I know you are discouraged. I am too, but we have a responsibility to those who might come. We will go on, and we will do the best job we possibly can. It is not the fault of those who come that others do not. They should not be punished with less than our best."

Heartened by his words, the minstrels gave their best performance ever. After the show, the old man called his troupe to him again. In his hand was a note handed to him by one of the audience members just before the doors closed behind him. Slowly the man read, "Thank you for a beautiful performance." It was signed simply, "Your King."

Even if no one else notices the quality of your work, God does. Do your best. Do it for Him!

Daniel was preferred above the presidents and princes, because an excellent spirit was in him.

DANIEL 6:3

During a prayer meeting one night, an elderly woman pleaded, "It really doesn't matter what You do with us, Lord, just have Your way with our lives." Adelaide Pollard, a rather well-known itinerant Bible teacher, overheard her prayer. At the time, she was deeply discouraged because she had been unable to raise the money she needed to go to Africa for missionary service. She was moved by this woman's sincere request of God, and when she went home that evening, she meditated on Jeremiah 18:3-4: *Then I went down to the potter's house, and, behold, he wrought a work on the wheels. And the vessel that he made of clay was marred in the hand of the potter: so he made it again another vessel, as seemed good to the potter to make it.*

> *Don't ask God for what you think is good; ask Him for what He thinks is good for you.*

Before retiring, Adelaide took pen in hand and wrote in hymn form her own prayer:

Have Thine own way, Lord! Have Thine own way!

Thou art the potter, I am the clay.

Mold me and make me after Thy will,

While I am waiting, yielded and still.

The best way to discover the purpose for your life is to give yourself, along with all your plans and dreams, to God. Then He can reveal and fulfill His plan for you. You won't be disappointed.

"This, then, is how you should pray: 'Our Father in heaven, hallowed be your name, your kingdom come, your will be done on earth as it is in heaven.'"

MATTHEW 6:9-10 NIV

Without God, the world would
be a maze without a clue.

Up in the choir loft of the old church on Main Street, there was an organ. In between holiday celebrations, it sat idle collecting dust—and mice. The mice that were born inside the organ considered their home a kind of quiet maze, filled with hammers, wires, and chimes—until Christmas Eve.

As the first notes from the slightly-off-tune instrument filled the home of the mice with music, they were awestruck. How their home moved and roared! What talent and timbre it possessed! But one small mouse wondered if there was more to the mystery. As he strained to pull himself through a small opening near the floorboards, he saw a woman carefully placing her fingers on the yellowed keys. The mouse realized it was the woman, not the organ itself, who possessed this wonderful gift of music. He ran back to tell everyone there was someone greater than the organ itself—someone who was making it sing!

The other mice laughed and laughed. Who could believe such a preposterous tale? After all, hadn't they seen the hammers move by themselves with their own eyes?

There's more to life, and truth, than meets the eye. So when someone tells you "seeing is believing," remember, *Faith is being sure of what we hope for and certain of what we do not see* (Hebrews 11:1 NIV).

This God is our God for ever and ever; he will be our guide even to the end.
PSALM 48:14 NIV

In 1970, Wally started baking chocolate chip cookies for his friends, using a recipe and procedure that had been passed down from his Aunt Della. For five years he gave away every batch he made, even though people often told him his cookies were so good he should go into business. Wally had other ideas though. He was determined to become a big-time show business manager.

Opportunities are seldom labeled.

Then one day a friend, B. J. Gilmore, told him that she had a friend who could put up the money for a cookie-making business. Her friend never made the investment, but Wally got some of his own friends—including Jeff Wall, Helen Reddy, and Marvin Gaye—to invest some money. Then he was off and running.

Originally, he intended to open only one store on Sunset Boulevard, just enough to "make a living." After all, his was the only store in the world dedicated to the sale of nothing but chocolate chip cookies. Business grew virtually overnight. Wally's "Famous Amos Chocolate Chip Cookies" were soon distributed worldwide. Wally himself became a spokesman for other products, from eggs to airlines, to a telephone company. While he once dreamed of managing stars, he is now one in his own right!

Sometimes dreams come through the back door. Keep it unlocked!

Seek, and ye shall find; knock,
and it shall be opened unto you.

MATTHEW 7:7

> *Don't be discouraged;*
> *everyone who got where he is,*
> *started where he was.*

Have you ever seen a flea circus? Though it certainly can't compare to a three-ring performance with trapeze artists and tiny cars filled with clowns, the mere fact that fleas can be trained is an entertaining concept. How trainable are fleas? Actually, what they learn is more of a result of conditioning through repetition, rather than training.

If you put fleas into a small box, they will continue to jump, hitting the top of the box over and over again. After awhile, they will stop jumping high enough to bump into the lid. In fact, they learn this lesson so well that if you then remove the lid, they still won't jump out of the box. They have conditioned themselves to jump only "so high."

Are there any areas in your life where you have conditioned yourself to jump only "so high"? Do you feel limited by your family background? By mistakes you've made in the past? By your socioeconomic status? Do you see yourself as a "C" student and expect nothing more? Do you think of yourself as a success or a failure? As creative or as unimaginative? As valuable or as insignificant? As a child of God or the result of chance? When it comes to how you view yourself, what you see is usually what you'll get. It's time to think outside the box. How high can you jump?

Though your beginning was insignificant,
Yet your end will increase greatly.

JOB 8:7 NASB

A number of definitions of maturity have been offered by experts, but these are perhaps among the best-understood by the average person:

- Maturity is when you want to have a puppy to call your own, AND you remember on your own to give it food and water every day.

- Maturity is when you know how to dress yourself, AND you remember to put your dirty clothes in the laundry hamper after you've taken them off.

- Maturity is when you are capable of using a telephone, AND you know how to keep your calls short so others can have access to the phone.

> *Maturity doesn't come with age; it comes with acceptance of responsibility.*

- Maturity is when you are old enough to stay at home alone, AND you can be trusted to have friends over.

- Maturity is when you are old enough to drive the car, AND you are responsible enough to pay for the gasoline you use.

- Maturity is when you are old enough to stay up late, AND you are wise enough to go to bed early.

If you want to know how mature you really are, measure your ability to take responsibility for your personal choices.

When I was a child, I spake as a child,
I understood as a child, I thought as
a child: but when I became a man,
I put away childish things.

1 CORINTHIANS 13:11

*The capacity to care gives
life its deepest significance.*

When Ryan found out his dog, Mulder, was going to have puppies, every morning was a race to the laundry room to see if the miracle had occurred while he slept. One morning, Ryan was rewarded by the sight of nine squirming balls of fur. Knowing that his parents had said he could keep only one, Ryan made the difficult choice of deciding which one would stay and which ones would be given away.

Six weeks later, Ryan made a cardboard sign that he carefully attached to the mailbox in front of his house. It read, "Cute puppies. FREE!" After several weeks, only two of the puppies had been given away, so Ryan decided to try a new approach. His new sign read, "Five cute puppies and only one really ugly one. Free to a good home!" The puppies were gone within the day. Every person who knocked on the door wanted to come to the rescue of that one poor, ugly pup.

Plenty of people want to help the underdog. Too often they're just not sure of how to go about it. Who has God put in your life that could use your help today? It could be a gift of time, finances, elbow grease, or maybe just friendship. Reaching out to help someone doesn't deplete your resources. It actually enlarges your capacity to care.

Carry each other's burdens, and in this way you will fulfill the law of Christ.

GALATIANS 6:2 NIV

A group of businessmen went to a remote mountain retreat for a weekend of leadership training. Expecting graphs, statistics, and pep talks, they were more than a little wary when they were asked to trade their notebooks in for shovels. Next, their boss, Mr. Clarkson, gave them their assignment for the weekend. "I want you to dig a ditch two feet wide and ten inches deep around the perimeter of the cabin." With those words, Mr. Clarkson walked back to the cabin and disappeared inside.

The easiest way to dignity is humility.

At first the group was silent, stunned by the ridiculous task that lay ahead. Soon, however, the silence turned into questioning the purpose of the exercise, arguing if nine inches was close enough to ten, and complaining about having risen to the top of the corporate ladder only to be forced to do manual labor. Finally, Bill, a newcomer to the group, turned to the others and said, "Who cares why we have to do this. Let's just do it and get it over with!"

With those words, the cabin door opened and Mr. Clarkson reappeared. "Gentlemen," he said as he grabbed Bill's hand, "I'd like you to meet your new vice-president."

The "whys" of what you have to do in life won't always be clear; but as long as you understand the "hows," the best thing to do is get to work.

"God sets himself against the proud, but he shows favor to the humble."

JAMES 4:6 NLT

The happiest people don't necessarily have the best of everything. They just make the best of everything.

A story is told of identical twins: one a hope-filled optimist who often said, "Everything is coming up roses," and the other, a sad and hopeless pessimist who continually expected the worst to happen. The concerned parents of the twins brought them to a psychologist in the hope that he might be able to help them balance the boys' personalities.

The psychologist suggested that on the twins' next birthday, the parents put them in separate rooms to open their gifts. "Give the pessimist the best toys you can afford," the psychologist said, "and give the optimist a box of manure." The parents did as he had suggested.

When they peeked in on the pessimistic twin, they heard him complaining, "I don't like the color of this toy. I'll bet this toy will break! I don't like to play this game. I know someone who has a bigger toy than this!"

Tiptoeing across the corridor, the parents peeked in and saw their optimistic son gleefully throwing manure up in the air. He was giggling as he said, "You can't fool me! Where there's this much manure, there's gotta be a pony!"

How are you looking at life today? As an accident waiting to happen, or a blessing about to be received?

I have learned, in whatsoever state I am, therewith to be content. . . . I can do all things through Christ which strengtheneth me.

PHILIPPIANS 4:11-13

Famous World War II general, George S. Patton Jr., was an avid reader and student of history. He wrote to his son in 1944: "To be a successful soldier, you must know history. Read it objectively. In Sicily, I decided, as a result of my information, observations, and instincts, that the enemy was not capable of initiating another large-scale attack. I bet my shirt on it and I was right."

Learn by experience— preferably other people's.

When he observed the situation in Normandy on July 2, 1944, Patton immediately wrote Eisenhower that the German Schlieffen Plan of 1914 could be applied. A month later, the operation brought about the German defeat in Normandy.

Patton's uncanny ability to predict the enemy's actions most likely was developed by thousands of hours of reading history. Historical parallels were constantly on his mind.

The book that perhaps influenced Patton most was Ardant du Picque's *Battle Studies.* Patton used it to help solve the problem of getting infantry to advance through enemy artillery fire.

If you are interested in being a success in life, immerse yourself in history, especially the life stories of successful people. Read it objectively. You will learn from the mistakes and failures of others, as well as their successes and triumphs.

All these things happened to them as examples—as object lessons to us—to warn us against doing the same things.
1 Corinthians 10:11 TLB

> *It's not hard to make decisions when you know what your values are.*

Justin looked at his math final with a sense of defeat. He just didn't get it. He knew he should have spent more time studying over the weekend. He also knew how disappointed his dad would be if he failed this class and had to repeat it next year. Justin glanced up at the clock to see how much longer he had to sit there, trying to look as though he was working.

Out of the corner of his eye, Justin saw Lynn working hard on her test right next to him. Lynn was Mrs. Mathison's star pupil. She set the grade curve for the entire class. If Justin moved just a bit to the right, he might be able to see a few answers—just enough to help him pass the final. His father's words kept echoing through Justin's head, *Honesty is always the best policy. Not the easiest, but the best.* Justin had heard those words since he was a little boy. Better to disappoint his father with the truth than try to please him with a lie. Justin looked back at his test and gave the answers another try.

When faced with a split-second decision, which way you go depends on what truth is planted deepest in your heart. Is there anything that would cause you to compromise your values? What and why?

> *Daniel purposed in his heart*
> *that he would not defile himself.*
> DANIEL 1:8

Jewish physician, Boris Kornfeld, was imprisoned in Siberia. There he worked in surgery, helping both the staff and prisoners. He met a Christian whose name is unknown, but whose quiet faith and frequent reciting of the Lord's Prayer had an impact on Dr. Kornfeld.

One day while repairing the slashed artery of a guard, Dr. Kornfeld seriously considered suturing the artery in such a way that the guard would slowly die of internal bleeding. The violence he recognized in his own heart appalled him, and he found himself saying, "Forgive us our sins as we forgive those who sin against us." Afterward, he began to refuse to obey various inhumane, immoral, prison-camp rules, even though he knew his quiet rebellion would place his life in danger.

> *I am only one; but still I am one. I cannot do everything, but still I can do something; I will not refuse to do the something I can do.*

One afternoon, he examined a patient who had undergone an operation to remove cancer. He saw in the man's eyes a depth of spiritual misery that moved him with compassion, and he told him his entire story, including a confession of his secret faith. That very night, Dr. Kornfeld was murdered as he slept; but his testimony was not in vain. The patient who heard his confession had become a Christian as a result. He survived the prison camp and went on to tell the world about life in the gulag.

That patient was Aleksandr Solzhenitsyn, who became one of the leading Russian writers of the twentieth century. He revealed to the world the horrors of the prison camps and perils of Russian communism.

You can make a difference. You can change your world. God has a wonderful plan for your life.

Under his (Christ's) direction the whole body is fitted together perfectly, and each part in its own special way helps the other parts.

EPHESIANS 4:16 TLB

Politeness goes far,
yet costs nothing.

Every patient on the fourth floor looked forward to Nurse Gustavson's shift. There was just something about her. Maybe it was the way she looked her patients in the eye when she spoke to them, or the fact that she always remembered their names, without first having to sneak a glance at their medical charts. How she could be both efficient and tender. Little did those patients on the fourth floor know that it hadn't always been that way.

Angie Gustavson had ever been an uncaring nurse—just overworked and overwhelmed. When she was diagnosed with breast cancer five years earlier, she found herself on the other side of the medical chart—and medical care. Even though she understood more about what was going on than the typical patient, she still felt frightened and alone. The hospital staff gave her medication to relieve her physical pain, but often her emotional pain was left unaddressed. That's when she knew that if she recovered, she could never look at patients the same way again. They were more than just an "appendicitis" or a "broken leg." They were mothers, fathers, brothers, sisters, and friends. They were people God dearly loved, and so should she.

How you treat people reflects how much you value them. Does the way you treat waitresses, telemarketers, and other drivers, reflect their true worth?

A kind man benefits himself.
PROVERBS 11:17 NIV

Connie thumbed through the same worn catalog. Another Saturday with nothing to do. She looked forward to spending time with friends on her days off, but apparently no one seemed to feel that way about her. Lately, the only ones who ever called were telemarketers.

We should behave to our friends as we would wish our friends to behave to us.

As lunchtime approached, Connie decided to head to the deli to pick up a sandwich. Connie spotted Susan as soon as she got up to the counter. *What was she doing working here?* Connie tried to head back out the door, not wanting to encounter her longtime friend who so obviously was avoiding her, but she had already caught Susan's eye.

"Connie!" Susan called out over the counter. "It's so good to see you! Ron lost his job a couple of weeks ago, so I'm working two jobs trying to catch up on bills. Have you heard anything from Rhonda?"

"No," Connie replied coldly. "I haven't heard anything from anyone."

"She's in the hospital, you know," Susan said quietly. "Maybe you should stop by for a visit. Things don't look all that good."

Connie's face turned red with shame. Here she was waiting around for her friends to reach out to her, when she should have been reaching out to them. Friendship is a two-way relationship. Is there someone you need to call today?

As ye would that men should do to you,
do ye also to them likewise.
LUKE 6:31

*Character is what
you are in the dark.*

In many ways, Ernest Shackleton's voyage to the Antarctic looked like a complete disaster. Shackleton and his crew had to cross 2,100 miles of frozen desolation to reach their destination of the South Pole. Within 93 miles of their goal, Shackleton decided that to journey further would endanger the lives of his entire crew. He ordered the crew to abandon the ice-locked "Endurance." Then they began their 200 mile trek across the Antarctic wasteland to where they could launch the lifeboat they were forced to drag with them. One thousand miles off shore lay South Georgia Island and their hope for survival.

In Shackleton's diary, he tells of the night they were down to one last ration of hardtack for each man. Some men ate their dry biscuit with a bit of tea, made from melted ice. Others stowed their ration in their food sack, not knowing what lay ahead. As Shackleton lay down to sleep, he noticed one of his crew opening another man's food sack. Shackleton was shocked that one of his most trusted men would consider stealing from a fellow crew member. As Shackleton watched, however, the man took his own precious hardtack and slipped it into his crew mate's sack.[9]

True heroes aren't just victorious in success. Sometimes, they shine brightest in the face of failure. What will it take to bring out the hero in you?

The integrity of the upright shall guide them.
PROVERBS 11:3

As a senior in high school, Jim batted an average of .427 and led his team in home runs. He was also quarterback of his football team, which made it to the state semifinals. Jim later became a pitcher for the New York Yankees.

That's a remarkable achievement for any athlete, but an almost unbelievable one for Jim, who was born without a right hand.

A little boy who had only parts of two fingers on one of his hands once came to Jim in the clubhouse after a Yankees' game and said, "They call me 'Crab' at camp. Did kids ever tease you?"

Adversity causes some men to break, others to break records.

"Yea," Jim replied. "Kids used to tell me that my hand looked like a foot." And then he asked the boy an all-important question, "Is there anything you can't do?" The boy answered, "No."

"Well, I don't think so either," Jim responded.

A limitation can only hold us back if we *think* it can. God certainly doesn't see us as limited, for He has given us unlimited potential. When we begin to see ourselves the way God sees us, there are no records we can't break!

If thou faint in the day of adversity, thy strength is small.

PROVERBS 24:10

Learn to say "No;" it will be of more use to you than to be able to read Latin.

When Amy Carmichael said no, she didn't do so out of laziness or selfishness. For more than fifty years, she worked with people from the lower castes in India, particularly young girls. Following a serious accident, she spent the last twenty years of her life directing her associates to carry on her work with the poor from her bedside. During that time, she authored thirteen books, in addition to the twenty-three she'd already written. Her life could be characterized by the courage to say yes to God and to living a life of self-sacrifice.

Along with Amy Carmichael's dedication and hard work, another reason for her success was her practice of "leaving a margin" in her life. She encouraged this practice with everyone she worked with, taking full advantage of it herself. Even amidst her busy schedule, she took time for reading, relaxation, and personal renewal. She knew when to say no. Do you?[10]

Is there anything that motivates you to say yes when you know you should be saying no? The fear of disappointing others? The need for a larger income? The desire to avoid confrontation? Just plain impulsiveness? If you say yes when your heart says no, do you follow through on your commitment; or do you procrastinate, make excuses, or fail, so you won't be asked again? Maybe it's time for "leaving a margin" in your life.

Just say a simple yes or no,
so that you will not sin.
JAMES 5:12 TLB

When Teddy Roosevelt was asked to give a speech to the Naval War College in Newport, Rhode Island, on June 2, 1897, his theme was "Readiness." He insisted the only way to keep peace was to be ready for war, and the only way to be ready for war was to enlarge the navy. It was a rousing, patriotic speech.

The following February, the *Maine* was blown up, killing 264 sailors, and Americans across the land cried, "Remember the *Maine!*" In April, President McKinley asked Congress to declare war.

Men are alike in their promises. It is only in their deeds that they differ.

For obvious reasons, Americans were not surprised that Roosevelt backed the war effort. Most Americans *were* surprised, however, when Teddy Roosevelt resigned from his position as assistant secretary of the navy three weeks after the war declaration so that he'd be ready to fight. His friends told him he was crazy for throwing away his political future. His wife was against it. Yet all who knew Roosevelt well knew their protests were in vain. He had to join the effort.

Roosevelt later wrote that he wanted to be able to tell his children why he had fought in the war, not why he *hadn't* fought in it. As far as he was concerned, a person simply couldn't preach one thing and then do another. It is this approach to life that will separate you from the pack and cause you to become a great man or woman.

Many a man claims to have unfailing love, but a faithful man who can find?

PROVERBS 20:6 NIV

111

> *Don't cross your bridges until you get to them. We spend our lives defeating ourselves crossing bridges we never get to.*

In 1863, New York's Brooklyn Bridge was a miracle in the making. Bridge-building experts from around the world advised engineer John Roebling that his plans could never succeed; but Roebling believed in his idea, and so did his son, Washington. Together they developed the innovative plans and hired their construction crew.

Just a few months after construction had begun, an accident on the site killed Roebling and left his son with permanent brain damage. Since only the Roeblings understood how the bridge was to be built, everyone assumed the project would be abandoned. But Washington had other plans. Unable to walk or talk, Washington's cognitive skills were still as sharp as ever. While in the hospital, he developed his own method of communication with his wife. Being able to move only one finger, he used it to tap out a code on his arm. He gave his wife instructions that she then passed on to the engineers in charge of completing the bridge. One day at a time, for thirteen years, Washington patiently tapped out instructions until the "miracle" bridge was finally completed.

Sometimes, an impossible dream is merely one that's been given up on too soon. Is there a goal that's looming larger than life in front of you? You're only responsible for what you can accomplish today. Don't give up. Get started!

"Don't be anxious about tomorrow.
God will take care of your tomorrow too.
Live one day at a time."
MATTHEW 6:34 TLB

In 1877, George Eastman dreamed that the wonderful world of photography might be accessible to the average person. At the time, photographers working outdoors had to carry multiple pieces of bulky equipment and a corrosive agent called silver nitrate. Eastman theorized that if he could eliminate most of this equipment, he would have something.

Working in a bank by day, he spent his nights reading books on chemistry and magazines about photography. He took foreign language lessons, so he could read information published in France and Germany. Then with a partner, he began his own company in 1881. Almost immediately, a problem arose with the new "dry plates" he had invented. Eastman refunded the money to those who had

You must have long-range goals to keep you from being frustrated by short-range failures.

purchased them and returned to his lab. Three months and 472 experiments later, he came up with the durable emulsion for which he had searched!

Eastman spent many nights sleeping in a hammock at his factory after long days designing equipment. To replace the glass used for photographic plates, he created a roll of thin, flexible material now known as film. To replace heavy tripods, he developed a pocket camera. By 1895, photography was at last available to the "common man."

George Eastman's long-term vision kept him motivated even when four hundred seventy one experiments failed. Keeping your ultimate dream in mind, set short, attainable goals, and before you even know it, your vision will be a reality!

Let us fix our eyes on Jesus, the author and
perfecter of our faith, who for the joy set before
him endured the cross, scorning its shame, and
sat down at the right hand of the throne of God.

HEBREWS 12:2 NIV

Clear your mind of can't.

Harry Houdini, who won fame as an escape artist early in the twentieth century, issued a challenge wherever he went. He claimed he could be locked in any jail cell in the country and set himself free within minutes. Indeed, he made good on this claim in every city he visited.

One time, however, something seemed to go wrong. Houdini entered a jail cell in his street clothes. The heavy metal doors clanged shut behind him, and he took from his belt a concealed piece of strong, but flexible metal. He set to work on the lock to his cell, but soon realized something was wrong. He worked for thirty minutes without success. An hour passed. This was much longer than it usually took to free himself. Houdini began to sweat and pant in exasperation. Still, he could not pick the lock.

Finally, after laboring for two hours, frustrated and barely fending off a sense of failure, Houdini leaned against the door. To his amazement, it swung open! It had never been locked in the first place!

How many times are challenges impossible simply because we think they are? When we focus our minds and energy on them and strike the word "can't" from our vocabulary, impossible tasks are almost always transformed into attainable goals.

I can do all things through Christ which strengtheneth me.

PHILIPPIANS 4:13

Grace Hopper was born with a desire to discover how things worked. At age seven, her curiosity led her to dismantle every clock in her childhood home! When she grew up, she eventually completed a doctorate in mathematics at Yale University. During World War II, Grace joined the navy and was assigned to the navy's computation project at Harvard University. There she met "Harvard Mark I," the first fully-functional, digital computing machine.

The future belongs to those who believe in the beauty of their dreams.

Unlike the clocks in her childhood home, "Harvard Mark I" had 750,000 parts and 500 miles of wire! While most experts believed computers were too complicated and expensive for anyone but highly trained scientists to use, Grace thought otherwise. Her goal was to understand how computers work and then to simplify the intimidating processes so more people could use them. Her work gave rise to the programming language COBOL.

As late as 1963, each large computer had its own unique master language. Grace became an advocate for a universally-accepted language. She had the audacity to envision a day when computers would be small enough to sit on a desk, more powerful than "Harvard Mark I;" and useful in offices, schools, and homes. At the age of seventy-nine, she retired from the U.S. Navy with a rank of rear admiral. More important to her, however, she had lived to see her dream of personal computers come true!

Believe in your dreams. With God, all things are possible.

"Anything is possible if you have faith."
MARK 9:23 TLB

> *The future belongs to those who see possibilities before they become obvious.*

ENIAC was one of the first computers to use electronic circuits, which made for lightning-fast calculations. At first, Thomas J. Watson Jr., the former chairman of IBM, saw no use for it. He said, "I reacted to ENIAC the way some people probably reacted to the Wright brothers' airplane. It didn't move me at all. I couldn't see this gigantic, costly, unreliable device as a piece of business equipment."

A few weeks later, he and his father wandered into a research office at IBM and saw an engineer with a high-speed punch-card machine hooked up to a black box. When asked what he was doing, the engineer replied, "Multiplying with radio tubes." The machine was tabulating a payroll at one-tenth the time it took the standard punch-card machine to do so. Watson was impressed. He and his dad liked the idea of having the world's first commercial electronic calculator.

That's how IBM entered the world of electronics. Within a year, they had electronic circuits that both multiplied and divided, and at that point, electronic calculators became truly useful. Thousands of IBM 604s were sold.

What wasn't yet obvious to Thomas Watson was obvious to the engineer working in the research department. Always keep your eyes and ears open; you never know what you might discover. Look for the possibilities around you.

The vision is yet for an appointed time . . .
it will surely come, it will not tarry.
HABAKKUK 2:3

How do you think most Olympic athletes spend their childhood? In swimming lessons, at wrestling matches, or running races? Williamette Rudolph spent her childhood in leg braces as a result of contracting polio as a young child. At the age of thirteen, once the braces, had been removed, Willie began running to strengthen her legs. She didn't stop once she caught up with the other kids, though. She kept on running until she became the fastest woman alive.

At the age of twenty, Willie won three gold medals in track in the 1960 Olympics. Though the victory she won over her physical challenges was remarkable, it wasn't the only battle she fought. Born into poverty to an African-American family, Willie

When I was a young man I observed that nine out of ten things I did were failures. I didn't want to be a failure, so I did ten times more work.

was the twentieth of twenty-two children; but she didn't let poverty, racism, or physical limitations shape her future. Instead, she turned possibilities into reality through hard work and keeping her eyes on the finish line.[11]

Just because something is difficult, doesn't make it impossible. Is there anything you've given up on in your life? Perhaps, it's breaking a habit or reaching a long-dreamed-of goal. Whatever it is, failure is only a sure thing once you've quit trying. Prayer, hard work, and perseverance are the keys to success. What's one goal in your life you could be more diligent in pursuing?

He becometh poor that dealeth with a slack hand: but the hand of the diligent maketh rich.

PROVERBS 10:4

Luck is a matter of preparation meeting opportunity.

We can learn a great deal from the Alaskan Bull Moose. Each fall during the breeding season, the males of the species battle for dominance. They literally go head-to-head, antlers crunching together as they collide. When the antlers are broken, defeat is ensured, since a moose's antlers are its only weapon.

Generally speaking, the heftiest moose with the largest and strongest antlers wins. Therefore, the battle is nearly always predetermined the summer before. It is then that the moose eat nearly 'round the clock. The one that consumes the best diet for growing antlers and gaining weight will be the victor. Those who eat inadequately will have weaker antlers and less bulk. The fight itself involves far more brawn than brain, and more reliance on bulk than on skill.

Many people stand around waiting for their "big break"—some extraordinary opportunity that will catapult them to success. Successful people, however, are almost always those who take the time and effort to prepare to seize opportunities when they present themselves. You won't find them sitting around waiting for a "break." You will find them studying, practicing, researching, developing, and honing their skills and talents. Take a lesson from the Alaskan Bull Moose—prepare today for tomorrow's opportunities.

Make the most of every opportunity.
COLOSSIANS 4:5 NIV

Albert Einstein is reputed to have had a wholesome disregard for the tyranny of custom. One evening, the president of Swarthmore College hosted a dinner held in Einstein's honor. He was not scheduled to speak, but after the award was made, the audience clamored "Speech, speech," and the president turned the podium over to him.

The most valuable of all talents is that of never using two words when one will do.

Einstein reluctantly came forward and said only this: "Ladies and gentlemen, I am very sorry but I have nothing to say," and then he sat down. A few seconds later, he stood up again and said, "In case I do have something to say, I'll come back."

Some six months later, Einstein wired the president of the college with this message: "Now I have something to say." Another dinner was scheduled, and this time, Einstein made a speech.

If you have nothing to say, it's wise to say nothing. If you do have something to say, it's wise to say it in as few words as possible. As the old saying goes, "If your mind should go blank, don't forget to turn off the sound."

In the multitude of words there wanteth not sin: but he that refraineth his lips is wise.

PROVERBS 10:19

> *Laziness is often mistaken*
> *for patience.*

Henry Ward Beecher, one of the most powerful preachers in American history, gave this illustration in one of his sermons:

"The lobster, when left high and dry among the rocks, has no sense and energy enough to work his way back to the sea, but waits for the sea to come to him. If it does not come, he remains where he is, and dies, although the slightest exertion would enable him to reach the waves, which are perhaps tossing and tumbling within a yard of him.

There is a tide in human affairs that casts men into 'tight places,' and leaves them there, like stranded lobsters. If they choose to lie where the breakers have flung them, expecting some grand billow to take them on its big shoulders and carry them to smooth water, the chances are that their hopes will never be realized."

Laziness is doing nothing, hoping nothing, being nothing. Patience on the other hand, means working on in hope that what you're waiting for will eventually come to pass, but you will continue to work on even if it doesn't.

Let us lay aside every weight, and the sin which doth so easily beset us, and let us run with patience the race that is set before us.
HEBREWS 12:1

A man who had been quite successful in the manufacturing business decided to retire. He called in his son to tell him of his decision, saying, "Son, it's all yours as of the first of next month." The son, while eager to take over the firm and exert his own brand of leadership, also realized what a big responsibility he was facing. "I'd be grateful for any words of advice you have to give me," he said to his father.

The father advised, "Well, I've made a success of this business because of two principles: reliability and wisdom. First, take reliability. If you promise goods by the tenth of the month, no matter what happens, you must deliver by the tenth. Your customers won't understand any delay. They'll see a delay as failure. So even if it costs you

One-half the trouble of this life can be traced to saying "yes" too quickly and not saying "no" soon enough.

overtime, double time, or golden time, you must deliver on your promise."

The son mulled this over for a few moments and then asked, "And wisdom?" The father shot back: "Wisdom is never making such a stupid promise in the first place."

Carefully weigh your ability to back up your words with evidence, and be sure you can deliver on a promise before you make it. A large part of your reputation is your ability to keep your word.

Seest thou a man that is hasty in his words? there is more hope of a fool than of him.
PROVERBS 29:20

I would rather fail in the cause that someday will triumph than triumph in a cause that someday will fail.

When Honorious was emperor of Rome, the great coliseum was often filled to overflowing with spectators who came from near and far to watch the state-sponsored games. Part of the sport consisted of human beings doing battle with wild beasts or one another—to the death. The assembled multitudes made a holiday of such sport and found the greatest delight when a human being died.

One such day, a Syrian monk named Telemachus was part of the vast crowd in the arena. Telemachus was cut to the core by the utter disregard he saw for the value of human life. He leaped from the spectator stands into the arena during a gladiatorial show and

132

cried out, "This thing is not right! This thing must stop!"

Because he had interfered, the authorities commanded that Telemachus be run through with a sword, which was done. He died—but not in vain. His cry kindled a small flame in the nearly burned-out conscience of the people, and within a matter of months, the gladiatorial combats came to an end.

The greater the wrong, the louder we must cry out against it. The finer the cause, the louder we must applaud.

Now thanks be unto God, which always causeth us to triumph in Christ.
2 CORINTHIANS 2:14

When Salvation Army officer Shaw saw the three men before him, tears sprang into his eyes. Shaw was a medical missionary who had just arrived in India. He had been assigned to a leper colony the Salvation Army was taking over. The three men before him had manacles and fetters binding their hands and feet. Their bonds were painfully cutting into their diseased flesh. Captain Shaw turned to the guard and said, "Please unfasten the chains."

"It isn't safe," the guard protested. "These men are dangerous criminals as well as lepers!"

Carve your name on hearts and not on marble.

"I'll be responsible," Captain Shaw said. "They are suffering enough." He then reached out, took the keys, knelt, tenderly removed the shackles from the men, and treated their bleeding ankles and wrists.

About two weeks later, Shaw had to make an overnight trip. He dreaded leaving his wife and child alone. The words of the guard came back to him, and he was concerned about the safety of his family. When Shaw's wife went to the front door the morning she was alone, she was startled to see the three criminals lying on her steps. One of them explained, "We know the doctor go. We stay here all night so no harm come to you."

Even dangerous men are capable of responding to an act of love! Touched lives are the most important monuments you can leave.

The only letter I need is you yourselves! . . . They can see that you are a letter from Christ, written by us. . . . not one carved on stone, but in human hearts.

2 CORINTHIANS 3:2-3 TLB

There is no poverty that can overtake diligence.

A young reporter once interviewed a successful businessman. The reporter asked the man to give him a detailed history of his company. As the man talked at length, the reporter began to be amazed by the great many problems the man had overcome. He finally asked him, "But how did you find the strength to overcome so much?"

The old gentleman leaned back in his chair and said, "There's really no trick to it." Then he added, "You know, there are some troubles that seem so high you can't climb over them." The reporter nodded in agreement, thinking of several he was currently facing. "And," the wise businessman went on, "there are some troubles so wide you can't walk around them."

Again, the reporter nodded. The man went on, raising his voice dramatically, "And there are some problems so deep you can't dig under them." Eager for a solution, the reporter said, "Yes? Yes?"

"It's then," the man concluded, "that you know the only way to beat the problem is to duck your head and wade right through it."

A problem rarely decreases in size while a person stands and stares at it. When you diligently pursue a solution, however, your problem is guaranteed to shrink.

He becometh poor that dealeth with a slack hand: but the hand of the diligent maketh rich.

PROVERBS 10:4

American sports fans watched in awe on Sunday, March 4, 1979, as Phil took to the giant-slalom slopes at Whiteface Mountain, New York. He exploded onto the course and then settled into a powerful carving of the mountainside.

Nonetheless, at gate thirty-five, tragedy struck. Phil hooked his inside ski on a pole, went flying head over heels, and crashed in a crumpled heap. The ski team physician described the injury as "the ultimate broken ankle"—a break of both the ankle and lower leg. He had to put the bones back together with a three-inch metal plate and seven screws.

Never despair; but if you do, work on in despair.

The question was not whether Phil would ever ski again, but if he would ever walk again. Looking back, Phil describes the months after his injury as a time of deep despair. Still, he never entertained doubts about walking or skiing.

After two months on crutches and a highly disciplined exercise program, he forced himself to walk without limping. In August, he began skiing gentle slopes. Less than six months after the accident, he entered a race in Australia and finished second. In February of 1980, less than a year after his agonizing injury, Phil Mahre took on the same mountain where he had fallen. This time, he won an Olympic silver medal.

When defeat and despair threaten to overtake you and squash your dreams, keep on going. Eventually, you will overtake defeat with victory and despair with joy!

As for you, be strong and do not give up,
for your work will be rewarded.
2 CHRONICLES 15:7 NIV

You can accomplish more in one hour with God than one lifetime without Him.

The Lord appeared to a man named Ananias in a vision and asked him to undertake what Ananias must surely have perceived as a dangerous mission. He directed him to go to the house of a man named Judas, lay his hands on a man named Saul of Tarsus, and pray that he might receive his sight. Saul had been blinded while traveling to Damascus to persecute the Christians there, having the full intent of taking them captive to Jerusalem for trial, torture, and death. Even so, Ananias did as the Lord asked him, and within the hour, Saul's sight was restored.

According to Christian legend, Ananias was a simple cobbler who had no idea what happened to Saul after that day, or how he had changed the course of human history by obeying God in a simple act that was part of Saul's transformation into the Apostle Paul. As he lay on his deathbed, Ananias looked up toward heaven and whispered, "I haven't done much, Lord: a few shoes sewn, a few sandals stitched. What more could be expected of a poor cobbler?"

The Lord spoke in Ananias' heart, "Don't worry, Ananias, about how much you have accomplished—or how little. You were there in the hour I needed you, and that is all that matters."

Being in the right place at the right time, even if it's only for one hour, can give you the opportunity to change history. In order to be there, you must simply listen and obey.

With God all things are possible.
MATTHEW 19:26

Tales of a monster in Loch Ness have been circulating in the Scottish Highlands since A.D. 565. Some eyewitnesses have described it as having horns. Others have claimed it bears antennae or a gaping red mouth. Still others have sworn it is camel-shaped. People love to speculate as to what it could be: a snake-like primitive whale, a long-necked aquatic seal, a floating plant mass, a plesiosaur—even a mirage.

If you don't stand for something, you'll fall for anything!

There have been several scientific studies of the 750-foot-deep lake, including a sonar survey, all of which have uncovered nothing. That hasn't kept tourists and locals alike from scanning the loch as they drive by in hopes of seeing something they can't explain.

Believing in Nessie means having faith in something that proof cannot substantiate. Some people feel believing in God takes that same kind of faith. After all, there are no photographs or even sonar scans that give the world a concrete image of God. The only likeness created in His image is man. Yet God's handiwork is just one of the "proofs" that an invisible God is alive and active in our physical world.

What is your faith based on? How you were raised? Intuition? Tradition? Personal experience? The Bible is filled with eyewitness accounts of God in action. If you had to write your own account, what would you say?

If you do not stand firm in your faith,
you will not stand at all.

ISAIAH 7:9 NIV

*Perseverance is a great element of success;
if you only knock long enough
and loud enough at the gate,
you are sure to wake up somebody.*

Country-music star Randy Travis and his manager, Lib, remember the lean days of his career—all 3,650 of them.

For ten years, Lib did whatever it took to keep her club open long enough for somebody to discover Travis' talent. For his part, Randy sang his heart out, and when he wasn't singing, he fried catfish or washed dishes in the kitchen. Then it happened. Everything seemed to click for him. He had a hit called "On the Other Hand," an album contract, a tour offer, and a movie deal. He was hot! Everyone seemed to be calling him an overnight success.

Travis notes, "We were turned down more than once by every label in Nashville; but I'm kind of one to believe that if you work at something long enough and keep believing, sooner or later it will happen."

In many instances in life, it's perseverance that makes the difference, but as the popular phrase states, you can "hang in there." Don't stop believing! Don't give up hope! Eventually the door will be opened.

Ask, and it shall be given you; seek, and ye shall find; knock, and it shall be opened unto you.
LUKE 11:9

Today, a trip to the Hawaiian island of Molokai sounds inviting, but one hundred years ago it was synonymous with a death sentence. Those who contracted the disfiguring, and usually fatal, disease of leprosy were exiled to the desolate island. Once they arrived, these outcasts found no hospital, doctors, or teachers—only other lepers who could empathize with their misery.

Only one man had the courage to join them in their exile. Father Damien came all the way from Belgium to provide spiritual comfort to those at the leper colony. He wasn't met with open arms, however. The people there mistrusted him. They weren't willing to socialize with him, let alone help him build a church. In his first ten years on the island,

Man cannot discover new oceans unless he has the courage to lose sight of the shore.

Father Damien found himself an outcast. Lonely and discouraged, he spent much of his time building caskets and digging graves for the hundreds of people who died each year from Hansen's Disease, as leprosy is now known.

Ironically, it was only when Father Damien himself contracted the disease that he was accepted by those he came to help. Through his persistent faith and hard work, the people of Molokai finally received the medical supplies they needed. Though Father Damien died six years later, his courageous acts of love provided a legacy of hope for those who were once regarded as hopeless.[12]

Peter got out of the boat, and walked on the water and came toward Jesus.

MATTHEW 14:29 NASB

> *Consider the postage stamp: its usefulness consists of the ability to stick to one thing till it gets there.*

In March of 1987, Eamon Coughlan was running in a qualifying heat at the World Indoor Track Championships in Indianapolis. The Irishman was the reigning world-record-holder at fifteen-hundred meters, and he was favored to win the race handily. Unfortunately, with two-and-a-half laps left to run, he was tripped and fell hard. Even so, he got up and with great effort, managed to catch the race leaders. With only twenty yards to go, he was in third place, which would have been good enough to qualify for the final race.

Then Coughlan looked over his shoulder to the inside. Seeing no one there, he relaxed his effort slightly. What he hadn't noticed, however, was that a runner was charging hard on the outside. This runner passed Coughlan just a yard before the finish line, thus eliminating him from the finals. Coughlan's great comeback effort ended up being worthless for one and only one reason: he momentarily took his eyes off the finish line and focused on the would-be competitors instead.

One of the most important factors in reaching your goals in life is to have a single-minded focus. Don't let yourself become distracted by what others do or say. Run your race to win!

I have fought a good fight, I have finished my course, I have kept the faith.
2 TIMOTHY 4:7

People often think of heart surgeons as being the arrogant prima donnas of the medical world. Those who know Dr. William DeVries, the surgeon who pioneered the artificial heart, couldn't *disagree* more. Co-workers at Humana Hospital Audubon in Louisville, Kentucky, describe DeVries as the kind of doctor who shows up on Sundays just to cheer up discouraged patients. He occasionally changes dressings, traditionally considered a nurse's job, and if a patient wants him to stick around and talk, he always does.

It needs more skill than I can tell to play the second fiddle well.

Friends say DeVries is an "old shoe" who fits in wherever he goes. He likes to wear cowboy boots with his surgical scrubs, and he often repairs hearts to the beat of Vivaldi or jazz. "He has always got a smile lurking," says Louisville cardiologist, Dr. Robert Goodin, "and he's always looking for a way to let it out."

No matter how high you rise, never forget that you started at ground zero. Even if you were born to great wealth and privilege, you still were once a helpless babe. Real success comes not in thinking you have arrived at a place where others should serve you; but in recognizing that in whatever place you are, you have arrived at a position where you can serve others.

He that is greatest among you
shall be your servant.
MATTHEW 23:11

151

A man never discloses his own character so clearly as when he describes another's.

After several months of romance, Napoleon and Josephine decided to marry. The notary who made out the marriage contract was one of Josephine's friends. He secretly advised her against marrying "an obscure little officer who has nothing besides his uniform and sword and has no future." He thought she should find someone of greater worth. With her charms, he advised, she might attract a wealthy man, perhaps an army contractor or a business investor.

Napoleon was in the next room while the notary was giving this advice to his beloved. He could hear every word that was said. Still, he did not disclose he had overheard. Years later, however, he had his revenge.

After his coronation as Emperor, this same notary appeared before him on a matter of business. At the conclusion of their appointment, Napoleon smiled and observed that Madame de Beauharnais—queen of France—had done very well, after all, to have married that "obscure little officer who possessed nothing besides his uniform and sword and had no future."

The notary was forced to agree that Madame, indeed, had done well. As for himself, he was still a notary!

Be careful before you pass judgment on another. You're revealing something about yourself, and your words may come back to bite you.

A good man out of the good treasure of the heart bringeth forth good things: and an evil man out of the evil treasure bringeth forth evil things.

MATTHEW 12:35

Although we do not have the original manuscripts of the New Testament, we do have more than 99.9 percent of the original text because of the faithful work of manuscript copyists over the centuries.

Copying was a long, arduous process. In ancient days, copyists did not sit at desks while writing, but rather stood or made copies while sitting on benches or stools, holding a scroll on their knees. Notes at the end of some scrolls tell of the drudgery of the work:

The greatest use of life is to spend it for something that will outlive you.

- "He who does not know how to write supposes it to be no labor; but though only three fingers write, the whole body labors."

- "Writing bows one's back, thrusts the ribs into one's stomach, and fosters a general debility."
- "As travelers rejoice to see their home country, so also is the end of a book to those who toil."

Even so, without the work of faithful copyists, we would not have the Scriptures today. As one scribe aptly noted: "There is no scribe who will not pass away, but what his hands have written will remain forever."

When you are choosing what you will do as your life's work, there are many things to consider. Don't underestimate the satisfaction that comes from knowing what you do today will touch lives long after you are gone.

"Store up for yourselves treasures in heaven, where moth and rust do not destroy, and where thieves do not break in and steal."

MATTHEW 6:20 NIV

155

Every man's work, whether it be literature, or music, or pictures, or architecture, or anything else, is always a portrait of himself.

On Easter Sunday in 1939, a free concert took place in front of the Lincoln Memorial that was heard by 75,000 people, not including the millions who listened via radio. This special performance was arranged by Eleanor Roosevelt for the American contralto, Marian Anderson. The reason Anderson was singing on the monument's steps, instead of Constitution Hall where she had originally been scheduled to perform, was that she was black.

This wasn't the first time Anderson has been turned away because of her race, yet she persevered with grace. The public outcry over how the Daughters of the American Revolution (DAR), who owned Constitution

Hall, had treated Anderson inspired sweeping changes throughout their organization. Four years later the DAR invited Anderson to perform a benefit concert for China Relief at Constitution Hall, and she accepted.

Anderson went on to become the first African-American to join the Metropolitan opera of New York City. She also became an alternate delegate to the United Nations. Over the next twenty-five years, she received the Presidential Medal of Freedom, a Congressional gold medal, the Eleanor Roosevelt Human Rights Award, and a Grammy Lifetime Achievement Award.[13]

It takes courage to follow your heart, especially in the face of unjust treatment. Is the opinion of others holding you back from achieving something God has given you the talent and desire to do?

As in water face reflects face,
So the heart of man reflects man.

PROVERBS 27:19 NASB

During a homecoming football game against rival Concordia, Augsburg College found itself losing miserably. Late in the fourth quarter, however, nose guard David Stevens came off the bench and sparked a fire. He initiated or assisted in two tackles, and when a Concordia player fumbled the ball, David fell on it. As he held the recovered ball high, the crowd roared. It was an unforgettable moment for Augsburg fans!

What we do on some great occasion will probably depend on what we already are; and what we are will be the result of precious years of self-discipline.

David Lee Stevens was born to a woman who had taken thalidomide, an anti-nausea drug given to many pregnant women in the early '60s. To the horror of many parents and physicians, it was soon clear that the drug causes severe birth defects. David's feet appeared where his legs should have started.

Abandoned by his mother, David was adopted by a foster family. Bee and Bill Stevens imposed strict rules of behavior on David, nurtured him, and loved him. They insisted he learn to do things for himself, and they never put him in a wheelchair. At age three, he was fitted with "legs."

In school, David became a student leader, made good grades, organized special events, and befriended new students. In high school, he not only played football, but baseball, basketball, and hockey. He became a champion wrestler. When offered handicap license plates, he refused them stating simply, "Those are for people who need them. I am not 'disabled.'"

David was taught to discipline himself, and so he was able to perform, in spite of his apparent handicap. Whatever obstacle may be in your way, self-discipline can help you either rise above it or plow right through it.

I keep under my body, and
bring it into subjection.
1 CORINTHIANS 9:27

> *Our deeds determine us, as much as we determine our deeds.*

In the fourth round of a national spelling bee in Washington, eleven-year-old Rosalie Elliot, a champion from South Carolina, was asked to spell the word *avowal.* Her soft Southern accent made it difficult for the judges to determine if she had used an *a* or an *e* as the next to last letter of the word. They deliberated for several minutes and also listened to tape-recorded playbacks, but they still couldn't determine which letter had been pronounced.

Finally the chief judge, John Lloyd, put the question to the only person who knew the answer. He asked Rosalie, "Was the letter an *a* or an *e*?"

Rosalie, surrounded by whispering young spellers, knew by now the correct spelling of the word. Without hesitation, she replied that she had misspelled the word and had used an *e*.

As she walked from the stage, the entire audience stood and applauded her honesty and integrity, including dozens of newspaper reporters covering the event. While Rosalie had not won the contest, she had definitely come out a winner that day.

We often think that who we are determines what we do. It is equally true that what you do today will determine, in part, who you become tomorrow.

Even a child is known by his actions,
by whether his conduct is pure and right.
PROVERBS 20:11 NIV

To crack the lily-white system of higher education in Georgia in the 1960s, black leaders decided they needed to find only two "squeaky-clean" students who couldn't be challenged on moral, intellectual, or educational grounds.

In a discussion about who might be chosen, Alfred Holmes immediately volunteered his son, Hamilton, the top black male senior in the city. Charlayne Hunter-Gault also stepped forward and expressed an interest in applying to the university. Georgia delayed admitting both boys on grounds it had no room in its dormitories, and the matter eventually ended up in federal court. Judge Bootle ordered the university to admit the two, who were qualified in every respect.

> *All virtue is summed up in dealing justly.*

Thus, segregation ended at the university level in that state, and soon, the nation.

Attorney General Robert Kennedy declared in a speech not long after: "We know that it is the law which enables men to live together, that creates order out of chaos; and we know that if one man's rights are denied, the rights of all are endangered."

Justice may be universal, but it always begins at the individual level.

He hath shewed thee, O man, what is good;
and what doth the LORD require of thee,
but to do justly, and to love mercy,
and to walk humbly with thy God?

MICAH 6:8

> *No matter what a man's*
> *past may have been,*
> *his future is spotless.*

Reuben reached for his razor, intending to end his life. To those around him, he seemed to have it made. After all, he was a sophomore at prestigious Yale University and the son of a wealthy banker. Inside, however, Reuben's despondency was growing. He tried to dull the pain with gambling, alcohol, and an active social life; but nothing seemed to help—except his mother's prayers.

"My mother, 427 miles away, was praying and praying that I would become a minister of the Gospel," Reuben Archer Torrey explained. "And though I had gotten over sermons and arguments and churches and everything else, I could not get over my mother's prayers."

That night, after years of turning his back on God, Torrey decided to turn to Him for help. The change in Torrey's life was dramatic. After graduating from Yale Divinity School, he went on to help establish the Moody Bible Institute and Biola University, as well as serve as a dynamic pastor, teacher, and author. The life Torrey attempted to cut short, God used to touch countless others for another fifty-four years. Even today, seventy-four years later, Torrey's work and words continue to have an impact on the world.[14]

What kind of impact will your life have? No matter what is in your past, God can take hold of your future. When He does, your life is guaranteed to make a difference in the world.

*Forgetting those things which
are behind, and reaching forth
unto those things which are before.*

PHILIPPIANS 3:13

Carrying her bucket of popcorn, Diane hurried into the theater. As the lights dimmed, she carefully climbed over feet, purses, and discarded candy wrappers toward an empty seat in the fifth row. "Just in time!" whispered to an elderly gentleman seated to her left. Even in the darkness, Diane could see the expression on his face was a kind one.

As the movie began, Diane grabbed a handful of popcorn. The man next to her smiled, then put his hand into the bucket, helping himself. Not wanting to cause a scene, Diane ignored him. *Perhaps he was senile,* she thought. Throughout the movie, Diane ate her popcorn, while the stranger continued to do the same. With one small handful of popcorn remaining, the man tilted the bucket her way,

One of life's great rules is this: The more you give, the more you get.

offering Diane what was left. She grabbed it, fuming inside over the man's brazenness.

When the movie ended, the man smiled once more, picked up the empty popcorn bucket, and headed out of the theater. As Diane reached for her purse, she discovered a full bucket of popcorn on the floor next to her. She'd been eating out of the man's bucket the entire time!

It's the size of your heart, not your income, that determines how easily you share with others. Is there anything holding you back from being more generous with what God's given you?

"Whatever measure you use in giving—large or small—it will be used to measure what is given back to you."

Luke 6:38 NLT

*Everything comes to him
who hustles while he waits.*

What do you do when your life is on hold? While you're waiting for that perfect job? To be accepted into college? To meet just the right mate? For that big break? Is waiting synonymous with inactivity? Consider this . . .

- While confined to Wartburg Castle, Martin Luther translated the *Bible* into German.

- During a thirteen year imprisonment, Sir Walter Raleigh wrote *The History of the World*.

- While under house arrest, Galileo wrote *Dialogues,* from which Sir Isaac Newton later developed his three laws of motion.

- Dante's master work, *The Divine Comedy,* was written while the author spent twenty years in exile under a death sentence.

- While incarcerated in a Bedford jail, John Bunyan wrote *Pilgrim's Progress.*

Chances are, you're not reading this from a prison cell; but waiting for circumstances to change can make you feel as though you're existing in one. Consider what would have happened if you'd spent your last school year just waiting around for what lay ahead after graduation. You would have flunked. You had to work while you were waiting to get where you are now.

No matter what your circumstances, you have two choices on how to spend your time— you can waste it or invest it. Every day brings new opportunities to grow and contribute to the world around you, regardless of your circumstances. How are you going to spend the gift of today?

We do not want you to become lazy, but to imitate those who through faith and patience inherit what has been promised.

HEBREWS 6:12 NIV

According to an old legend, two monks named Tanzan and Ekido were traveling together down a muddy road. Heavy monsoon rains had saturated the area, and they were grateful for a few moments of sunshine to make their journey. Before long, they came around a bend and encountered a lovely girl in a silk kimono. She looked extremely forlorn as she stared at the muddy road before her.

At once, Tanzan responded to her plight. "Come here, girl," he said. Then lifting her in his arms, he carried her over the slippery ooze and set her down on the other side of the road.

As they went on their way, Tanzan noticed that Ekido was uncharacteristically silent. It was apparent that something was bothering

God has nothing to say to the self-righteous.

him deeply, but try as he would, Tanzan couldn't get Ekido to talk to him. Then that night after they reached their intended lodging, Ekido could no longer restrain his anger and disappointment. "We monks don't go near females," he said to Tanzan in an accusing voice. "We especially don't go near young and lovely maidens. It is dangerous. Why did you do that?"

"I left the girl back there, Ekido," replied Tanzan. "Are you still carrying her?"

God is not pleased when we practice the letter of the law without regard for the spirit behind it. Christ has established a new law—the law of love. That should always be our model for right living.

We have believed in Christ Jesus, that we might be accepted by God because of our faith in Christ. . . . For no one will ever be saved by obeying the law.

GALATIANS 2:16 NLT

> *Defeat is not the worst*
> *of failures. Not to have*
> *tried is the true failure.*

There once was a young man who lived a most miserable life. Orphaned before he was three, he was taken in by strangers. He was kicked out of school, suffered from poverty, and as the result of inherited physical weaknesses, he developed serious heart trouble as a teenager. His beloved wife died early in their marriage. He lived as an invalid most of his adult life, and he eventually died at the young age of forty. By all outward appearances, he lived a life doomed to defeat and obscurity.

Even so, he never quit trying to express himself and achieve success. During a twenty-year period, he produced some of the most brilliant articles, essays, and criticisms ever written. His poetry is still read widely and studied by virtually every high school student in the United States. His short stories and detective stories are well known. One of his poems, on display at the famous Huntington library in California, has been valued at more than fifty-thousand dollars, which is far more than the young man earned in his entire lifetime.

His name? Edgar Allan Poe.

Circumstances don't affect your chances for success nearly as much as your level of effort!

Be strong and of a good courage; be not afraid, neither be thou dismayed: for the LORD thy God is with thee withersoever thou goest.

JOSHUA 1:9

After falling twice in the 1988 Olympic speed-skating races, Dan Jansen sought out sports psychologist Dr. Jim Loehr, who helped him find a new balance between his sport and his life. He also helped Jansen learn to focus on the mental aspects of skating.

Peter Mueller became his coach, putting him through workouts that Dan has since described as the "toughest I've ever known." By the time the 1994 Olympics arrived, Jansen had more confidence than ever. He had set a 500-meter world record just two months earlier. The Olympic title in that event seemed to belong to him!

Unless you try to do something beyond what you have already mastered, you will never grow.

Unfortunately, Jansen fell during the five-hundred-meter race. He was disappointed and shaken, but Dr. Loehr immediately advised, "Start preparing for the one thousand-meter race. The five-hundred-meter is gone. Put it behind you."

The problem was that the 1,000-meter was Jansen's weakest event. He had always felt he couldn't win at that distance. Now it was his last chance for an Olympic medal. As the race began, Jansen said, "I just seemed to be sailing along," and then he slipped and came within an inch of stepping on a lane marker. Still, he resisted the urge to panic and raced on, attaining a world-record time that won him the gold medal!

It's a safe feeling to stick with those areas you have mastered and feel confident about. If you stay there, however, you will not grow. Seek out opportunities to master new skills and reach new goals. Don't be intimidated! With a strong mental attitude, your weakest event can become your greatest triumph.

Reaching forth unto those things which are before, I press toward the mark for the prize of the high calling of God in Christ Jesus.
PHILIPPIANS 3:13-14

I don't know the secret to
success, but the key to failure
is to try to please everyone.

It was a sunny, spring morning at Main Street Community Church. As Pastor Johnson walked to the front of the sanctuary, a single cough was heard from the choir loft. It was accompanied by the rustle of children adjusting in their seats and the sound of hymnals being returned to their places. The Sunday sermon was about to begin.

"Today, brothers and sisters, we are speaking about honesty," Pastor Johnson said with a smile. "Our text will be from the twenty-sixth chapter of Mark, verse six. How many of you are familiar with this famous passage?" Several hands were raised over the heads of the congregation. "You are the people I'd like to address my sermon to this morning,"

Pastor Johnson continued. "After all, the book of Mark only contains sixteen chapters."

Who are you when nobody's looking? Does that person bear any resemblance to who you are when you're the center of attention? If your personality resembles that of a chameleon, changing your appearance to fit in with your surroundings, it's time to ask yourself, *Who am I trying to please?* Being honest with those around you means more than just telling the truth. It means living it. Is there anyone you feel the need to impress? Why? How do you think God feels when you try to be someone other than who He created you to be?

Am I now trying to win the approval of men, or of God?

GALATIANS 1:10 NIV

The engineers hired to build a suspension bridge across the Niagara River faced a serious problem: how to get the first cable from one side of the river to the other. The river was too wide to throw the cable to the other side and too swift to cross by boat.

An engineer finally came up with a solution! With a favoring stiff wind, a kite was lofted and allowed to drift over the river and land on the opposite shore. Attached to the kite was a light string, which was threaded through the kite's tip so that both ends of the string were in the hands of the kite flyer. Once the kite was in the hand of engineers on the far side, they removed the kite from its string and set up a pulley. A small rope was attached to one end of the original kite string and pulled

Kites rise highest against the wind, not with it.

across the river. At the end of this string, a piece of rope was attached and pulled across and so on, until a cable strong enough to sustain the iron cable, which supported the bridge, could be drawn across the water.

Let your faith soar like that kite! Release it to God, believing that He can and will help you. When you link your released faith with patience and persistence, you will have what it takes to tackle virtually any problem.

When the way is rough, your patience has a chance to grow. So let it grow, and don't try to squirm out of your problems.

JAMES 1:3-4 TLB

The secret of success is to be like a duck—
smooth and unruffled on top, but
paddling furiously underneath.

Ellen Burstyn, a Tony Award-winning actress, once had a memorable acting lesson that she enjoys relating to those who question her about stage fright:

One day on Broadway, I became aware of a stir in the audience. Suddenly, I saw it! A stray cat was nonchalantly crossing the stage.

The cat stopped and turned toward the darkness of the audience and seemed startled to discover that the darkness was alive. She had presence, as though there were a thousand pairs of eyes out there, which, of course, there were. That realization stopped the cat dead in her tracks. Then she fled into the wings. I remember thinking, *I know just how she feels.*

I've often told this story to young actors because I think it shows that the job of the actor is to make contact with the kitty inside each of us—the one that wants to turn and run when it feels those thousand pairs of eyes on it. And to find the way to quiet the kitty and just go on doing what we have to do.[15]

Feeling frightened or nervous is not a sign of impending failure. It is a sign that you consider the performance ahead to be worth doing and doing well! Keep your eyes on your goal and remember those who will benefit from your work. This focus will calm your fears and fill you with purpose.

*His peace will keep your thoughts
and your hearts quiet and at rest
as you trust in Christ Jesus.*

PHILIPPIANS 4:7 TLB

A little boy was once overheard talking to himself as he strutted out of his house into the backyard, carrying a baseball bat and ball. Once in the yard, he tipped his baseball cap to his eager puppy, and picking up the bat and ball, he announced with a loud voice, "I'm the greatest hitter in the world."

He then proceeded to toss the ball into the air, swing at it, and miss. "Strike one!" he cried, as if playing the role of umpire.

The boy picked up the ball, threw it into the air, and said again, "I'm the greatest baseball hitter ever!" Again he swung at the ball and missed. "Strike two!" he announced to his dog and the yard.

Undaunted, he picked up the ball, examined his bat, and then just before tossing the ball

The cheerful man will do more in the same time, will do it better, will preserve it longer, than the sad or sullen.

into the air, announced once again, "I'm the greatest hitter who ever lived." He swung the bat hard, but missed the ball for the third time. "Strike three!" he cried. Then he added, "Wow! What a pitcher! I'm the greatest pitcher in all the world!"

An upbeat, positive mental attitude paves the way for a productive and satisfying life.

When a man is gloomy, everything seems to go wrong; when he is cheerful, everything seems right!

PROVERBS 15:15 TLB

> *Money is a good servant*
> *but a bad master.*

At the age of twenty-four, financial advisor and author Ron Blue felt he had everything he needed to be successful—an MBA degree, a CPA certificate, and a prestigious position in the New York City office of the world's largest CPA firm. At the age of thirty-two, he committed his life to Jesus Christ and gained a new perspective.

When Blue decided to establish his own financial advisory firm, he used his skills to develop a business plan and arrange for a ten-thousand-dollar line of credit at a bank. Almost immediately, however, he felt convicted that God did not want him to borrow money to start his business. He canceled the credit line, not knowing what to do next but knowing he was not to go into debt.

One day, while explaining his business idea to a friend, the friend said, "Would you consider designing a financial seminar for our executives who are getting ready to retire?" Ron jumped at the opportunity. His friend was the training director for a large company, and the company agreed to pay six thousand dollars in advance for development of the seminar, then one thousand dollars each for four seminars during the year. Ron had the ten thousand dollars he needed without borrowing a dime.

Do your best to stay out of debt. You'll feel much freer, and God will bless you for trusting in Him.

The rich ruleth over the poor, and the borrower is servant to the lender.

PROVERBS 22:7

Nelson Diebel, a hyperactive and delinquent child, was enrolled in the Peddie School where he met swimming coach Christ Martin, who believed the more one practices, the better one performs. Within a month, he had Nelson swimming thirty to forty hours a week, even though Nelson could not sit still in a classroom for fifteen minutes.

Martin saw potential in Nelson. He constantly put new goals in front of the boy, trying to get him to focus and turn his anger into strength. Nelson eventually qualified for the Junior Nationals, and from there, the Olympic trials.

No plan is worth the paper it is printed on unless it starts you doing something.

Then disaster struck. Nelson broke both hands and arms in a diving accident, and doctors warned he probably would never regain his winning form. Martin said to him, "You're coming all the way back. If you're not committed to that, we're going to stop right now." Nelson agreed, and within weeks after his casts were off, he was swimming again.

In 1992, Nelson Diebel won an Olympic gold medal. As he accepted his medal, he recalls thinking: *I planned and dreamed and worked so hard and I did it!* The kid who once couldn't sit still and who had no ambition had learned to make a plan, pursue it, and achieve it. He had become a winner in far more than swimming!

Dream big dreams! Then establish a plan, and stick with it! The possibilities are limitless.

Be ye doers of the word, and not hearers only, deceiving your own selves.

JAMES 1:22

*Life is a coin. You can spend
it any way you wish, but
you can spend it only once.*

Ann Scheiber and Hetty Green had a lot in common. Both of them lived frugal lives and left behind a fortune. Scheiber lived in a tiny, rundown apartment; but she was a financial wizard. Over the course of her lifetime, she turned a $5,000 investment into a $20 million fortune.

Hetty Green was once the richest woman in the United States, but no one could tell by looking at her. Instead of buying new clothes, Green would pad the old ones with newspaper to keep out the winter chill. She'd sell old rags to the junk man for change. Even though she owned two railroads, she'd sit up all night in coach, instead of paying for a bunk. Upon her death, she left behind a $75 million estate.[16]

Scheiber and Green were both wealthy women on the outside; but inside, they were poverty stricken. Both lived alone, had no friends, and left behind everything for which they'd worked so hard, to people they'd never even met. When you die, the most important things you'll leave behind are not those written up in your will. They're the love you've shared, the memories you've made, and the legacy of a life well-lived. If you were to die tonight, how would your friends remember you? What would God think about the way you're living your life?

It is appointed unto men once to die,
but after this the judgment.
HEBREWS 9:27

The German sculptor, Dannaker, worked for two years on a statue of Christ until it looked perfect to him. He called a little girl into his studio, and pointing to the statue, he asked her, "Who is that?" The little girl promptly replied, "A great man."

Dannaker was disheartened. He took his chisel and began anew. For six long years, he toiled. Again, he invited a little girl into his workshop, stood her before the figure, and said, "Who is that?" She looked up at it for a moment, and then tears welled up in her eyes as she folded her hands across her chest and said, "Suffer the little children to come unto me" (Mark 10:14). This time Dannaker knew he had succeeded.

Only passions, great passions, can elevate the soul to great things.

The sculptor later confessed that during those six years, Christ had revealed Himself to him in a vision, and he had only transferred to the marble what he had seen with his inner eyes.

Later, when Napoleon Bonaparte asked him to make a statue of Venus for the Louvre, Dannaker refused. "A man," he said, "who had seen Christ can never employ his gifts in carving a pagan goddess. My art is henceforth a consecrated thing."

The true value of a work comes not from effort, nor its completion, but from Christ who inspires it.

Fervent in spirit; serving the Lord.
ROMANS 12:11

*Failures want pleasing methods,
successes want pleasing results.*

Sadie Delaney's father taught her always to strive to do better than her competition. She proved the value of that lesson shortly before she received her teaching license. A supervisor came to watch her and two other student teachers. Their assignment was to teach a class to bake cookies. Since the supervisor didn't have time for each teacher to go through the entire lesson, she divided the lesson, and Sadie was assigned to teach the girls how to serve and clean up.

The first student teacher panicked and forgot to halve the recipe and preheat the oven. The second girl was so behind because of the first girl's errors that the students made a mess in forming and baking the cookies. Then it was

Sadie's turn. She said to the girls, "Listen, we have to work as a team."

They quickly baked the remaining dough. Several girls were lined up to scrub pans as soon as the cookies came out of the oven. Within ten minutes, they had several dozen perfect cookies and a clean kitchen. The supervisor was so impressed, she offered Sadie a substitute teacher's license on the spot. Sadie soon became the first black person ever to teach domestic science in New York City's public high schools.

Even when you have every right to blame others who have gone before you, don't make excuses. Do what it takes to get the job done!

No discipline seems pleasant at the time, but painful. Later on, however, it produces a harvest of righteousness and peace for those who have been trained by it.

HEBREWS 12:11 NIV

In the Topkapi Palace in Istanbul, Turkey, there is a set of antique dinnerware once used exclusively for royalty. Years ago, these unique plates were considered a kind of royal insurance policy. If the plate's green glaze turned red, that meant that the food that had been placed on it contained cyanide. Any plot to poison the sultan would instantly be revealed. Though modern-day scientists have analyzed the unique glaze, they cannot seem to duplicate its effects.

> *Once a word has been allowed to escape, it cannot be recalled.*

If only our words could send up such an obvious red flag. All too often, words are said in haste or anger. They may be spoken in a split second, but their effects can last a lifetime, causing damage that can poison a relationship . . . "You're so stupid!" "If you just lost some weight you could get a date." "I never loved you."

Has anything been said to you that still echoes through your head? Forgiving isn't an easy thing to do, but it's a necessary one if you want the ringing to stop. Are there words you've said to others that you know may still be replaying in their heads and hearts? You have the power to help turn that tape off. Have the courage to ask for forgiveness. Then ask God to help you use your words as a gift, instead of a weapon.

Let no corrupt communication proceed out of your mouth, but that which is good to the use of edifying, that it may minister grace unto the hearers.

EPHESIANS 4:29

Most of the things worth doing in the world were declared impossible before they were done.

Consider these examples of resistance to ideas and inventions that we now consider commonplace:

- In Germany, experts proved that if trains went as fast as fifteen miles an hour—considered a frightful speed—blood would spurt from the travelers' noses and passengers would suffocate when going through tunnels. In the United States, experts said the introduction of the railroad would require the building of many insane asylums, since people would be driven mad with terror at the sight of the locomotives.

- The New York YWCA announced typing lessons for women in 1881, and vigorous protest erupted on the grounds that the female constitution would break down under the strain.

- When the idea of iron ships was proposed, experts insisted that they would not float, that they would damage more easily than wooden ships when grounding, that it would be difficult to preserve the iron bottom from rust, and that iron would play havoc with compass readings.

- New Jersey farmers resisted the first successful cast-iron plow invented in 1797, claiming that the cast iron would poison the land and stimulate the growth of weeds.

Don't let the word *impossible* stop you. If inventors and visionaries left every impossible task undone, our lives would be considerably more difficult. Nothing worth doing is impossible with the help of God!

With God all things are possible.
MATTHEW 19:26

During the darkest days of the Civil War, the hopes of the Union nearly died. When certain goals seemed unreachable, the leaders of the Union turned to President Abraham Lincoln for solace, guidance, and encouragement. When a delegation called at the White House and detailed a long list of crises facing the nation, Lincoln told this story:

> Years ago a young friend and I were out one night when a shower of meteors fell from the clear November sky. The young man was frightened, but I told him to look up in the sky past the shooting stars to the fixed stars beyond, shining serene in the firmament, and I said, "Let us not mind the meteors, but let us keep our eyes on the stars."

Obstacles are those frightful things you see when you take your eyes off the goal.

When times are troubled or life seems to be changing too fast, keep your inner eyes of faith and hope on those things that you know to be lasting and sure. Don't limit your gaze to what you know or who you know, but focus on Whom you know—God alone. A relationship with Him is the supreme goal. He never changes, and He cannot be removed from His place as the King of glory.

Peter . . . walked on the water toward Jesus. But when he looked around at the high waves, he was terrified and began to sink.

MATTHEW 14:29-30 TLB

A good reputation is more valuable than money.

In *Up from Slavery,* Booker T. Washington describes meeting an ex-slave from Virginia:

I found that this man had made a contract with his master two or three years previous to the Emancipation Proclamation. The slave was to be permitted to buy himself, by paying so much per year for his body; and while he was paying for himself, he was to be permitted to labor where and for whom he pleased. Finding that he could secure better wages in Ohio, he went there.

When freedom came, the man was still in debt to his master some three hundred dollars. Notwithstanding that the Emancipation Proclamation freed him from any obligation to his master, this black man walked back to where his old master lived in Virginia, and placed the last dollar, with interest, in his hands.

In talking to me about this, the man told me that he knew that he did not have to pay his debt, but that he had given his word to his master, and he had never broken his word. He felt that he could not enjoy his freedom till he had fulfilled his promise.

Your ability to keep your word, not your ability to acquire money, is your true measure as a person!

A good name is rather to be chosen than great riches.

PROVERBS 22:1

Remember the story of *The Emperor's New Clothes?* Two unscrupulous con men convince the emperor that they can fashion for him an exquisite set of clothing. Best of all, they explain, only those who are wise and worthy of their position will be able to see the magical cloth the men will so skillfully tailor.

When the much antici- pated outfit is completed, the emperor realizes, to his dismay that *he* cannot see the clothing the swindlers have supposedly dressed him in. He panics, believing he must be both a fool and unworthy of ruling his kingdom. Trying to hide this fact from his subjects, he pretends he can see an outfit that doesn't exist. It takes a little boy, unconcerned about what others will think, to point out to the emperor

An error doesn't become a mistake until you refuse to correct it.

and the rest of the kingdom that the royal ruler is parading around in his underwear.

Everybody blows it now and then, but trying to cover up your mistakes can result in even greater embarrassment than just acknowledging them. When you do something wrong, have the integrity to admit it. Ask forgiveness from God and anyone you may have offended. Then move on. A mistake doesn't have to be a disaster. It can be an excellent teacher that prevents you from doing the same thing over again.

He who heeds discipline shows the way to life, but whoever ignores correction leads others astray.

PROVERBS 10:17 NIV

Hating people is like burning down your own house to get rid of a rat.

Once upon a time, there was a clown who forgot how to laugh. Perhaps it was the pressure of having to make others laugh day after day. Maybe, it was the fact that after years of being a clown, he seemed to know how every joke would end, before the punch line was reached. Whatever the reason, the clown hid in his dressing room, dreading the evening performance.

As he sat there with a heavy heart and a frown on his face, he took a good look at himself in the mirror. He saw a forty-year-old man with his face painted white, giant red lips, and yellow stars around each eye. He wore a tiny pointed cap, perched sideways on his receding hairline. As he eyed the rainbow ruffle around his collar and the red shoes twice the size of his feet, he was surprised by an unexpected chuckle—then another and another. Soon he was laughing so hard that tears were running down the blue stars on his cheeks. He thought to himself, *Whatever could possess a grown man to dress like this as a profession?*

It's been said that "those who can laugh at themselves will never cease to be amused." Don't take yourself so seriously that you forget to exercise your funny bone. Keeping it in shape will help keep your spirits high when life gets tough.

If ye bite and devour one another, take heed that ye be not consumed one of another.

GALATIANS 5:15

A missionary from Sweden was once urged by his friends to give up his idea of returning to India, because it was so hot there. "Man," the fellow Swede urged, as if telling his friend something he didn't already know, "it's 120 degrees in the shade in that country!" The Swedish missionary replied, "Vell, ve don't alvays have to stay in the shade do ve?"

Humor is not a sin. It is a God-given escape hatch. Being able to see the lighter side of life is a virtue. Every vocation and circumstance of life has a lighter side, if we are only willing to see it. Whole-some humor can do a great deal to help defuse a tense, heated situation. In developing a good sense of humor, we must be able to laugh at our own mistakes; accept justified criticism; and learn

Laughter is the sun that drives winter from the human face.

to avoid using statements that are unsuitable, even though they may be funny.

James M. Gray and William Houghton—two godly men—were praying together one day, and the elderly Dr. Gray concluded his prayer by saying, "Lord, keep me cheerful. Keep me from becoming a cranky, old man."

Keeping a sense of humor is a great way to become a sweet, patient, and encouraging person. Learn to laugh at yourself occasionally!

A merry heart maketh a cheerful countenance: but by sorrow of the heart the spirit is broken.

PROVERBS 15:13

Good nature begets smiles, smiles beget friends, and friends are better than a fortune.

What kind of woman receives proposals from a thousand men, including farmers, fishermen, vagrants, and millionaires? An heiress? A rock star? A beauty queen?

Evangeline Booth was none of those things. She was the head of the Salvation Army in the early 1900s. Born on Christmas day in 1865, Evangeline was the daughter of the Salvation Army's founder, William Booth. Even at an early age, her vision was the same as her father's—to help the poor and draw them closer to God. In turn, others seemed to be drawn to her.

What was the secret of her popularity? "I live for others," Evangeline once told a reporter. "My deepest desire is to make every person I meet a little better because I have passed this way." Even after her seventieth birthday, Evangeline was receiving so many marriage proposals by mail that her secretary finally quit showing them to her.[17]

Some people may be drawn to you because of your wit, your intelligence, your looks, or your bank account—for awhile, anyway. In the long run though, the most attractive feature you can possess is a deep love and concern for those around you. Today, what can you do to make the life of every person you meet a little better just because you happened to pass through it?

The light in the eyes [of him whose heart is joyful] rejoices the hearts of others.

PROVERBS 15:30 AMP

An American received a medical degree from New York University College of Medicine and earned an appointment to the Virus Research Laboratory at the University of Pittsburgh. Among the many honors he received for his work was a Presidential Medal of Freedom.

Jonas Salk, however, is not known for what he received, but for what he gave. He and his team of researchers gave their efforts to prepare an inactivated polio virus that could serve as an immunizing agent against polio. By 1952 they had created a vaccine. In 1955 the vaccine was released for widespread use in the United States, virtually ending the ravaging, crippling effects of polio.

No person was ever honored for what he received. Honor has been the reward for what he gave.

You will receive many opportunities in your life, and most likely a number of certificates, diplomas, and awards. What will ultimately count, though, is what you do with the training you have received and the skills and traits you have developed.

Find a way to give, create, or generate something today that will benefit others. Your actions may or may not bring you fame, but they will certainly bring you a sense of personal satisfaction—the greatest reward of all.

The righteous give without sparing.
PROVERBS 21:26 NIV

> *The difference between the right word and the almost right word is the difference between lightning and the lightning bug.*

Companies spend countless dollars on advertising, hiring creative professionals to come up with just the right words to sell their products to the public. Unfortunately, "just the right word" in English may give the wrong message when translated into a different language. Consider these international *faux pas:*

- When Pepsi's "Come alive with the Pepsi Generation" campaign went to China, the slogan was translated "Pepsi brings your ancestors back from the grave."

- Coca-Cola's luck wasn't much better. In Chinese, the name "Coca-Cola" sounds like "bite the wax tadpole" or "female horse stuffed with wax," depending on the dialect. After researching 40,000 characters, Coke altered the pronunciation of their name to "ko-kou-ko-le." This translated into the much more appetizing "happiness in the mouth."

- When the Pope visited Miami, tee-shirts were printed for the Spanish market which, when translated read, "I saw the potato" (la papa) instead of the Pope (el Papa).

- Clairol tried to introduce their "Mist Stick" curling iron into Germany. Unfortunately, "mist" is slang for manure in German. The "Manure Stick" was not a big seller.

Saying what you mean doesn't always come easily, even when you're just speaking your native language. It's easy enough to talk, but to say something worth listening to takes thought and a good listening ear. Why not make your words count by saying only what benefits those hearing it?

A word fitly spoken is like apples of gold in pictures of silver.

PROVERBS 25:11

Sophie knew her old textbooks were in the crawlspace, but "where in the crawlspace" was another question. If she planned to finish this article, Sophie knew she needed that history book she'd stashed away. Taking a flashlight, she opened the small door in the basement.

A scream caught in Sophie's throat. Long white tentacles reached out of the crawlspace and seemed to be trying to grab her flashlight—or her throat. Sophie slammed the door and ran back upstairs. After her heart had almost returned to a normal rhythm, Sophie was ready to analyze the situation from a reasonable perspective. Monsters were something kids imagined under their beds. Reasonable adults did not slam crawlspace doors on them.

This world belongs to the man who is wise enough to change his mind in the presence of facts.

Timidly, but with renewed determination, Sophie made her way back to the basement. She took a deep breath, ready to jump backwards if necessary, and then quickly opened the door.

The tentacles reached out toward her once more, but this time she paused to give them a closer look. They were growing out of a burlap sack of potatoes she'd left in the crawlspace months before. So much for monsters.

First impressions are not always accurate. Before forming a negative opinion about something or someone, take time to review the facts. Give second chances. Get a second opinion. Then, if the facts merit it, exercise enough courage to change your mind.

Whoever heeds correction gains understanding.
PROVERBS 15:32 NIV

Good words are worth much and cost little.

One day a young altar boy was serving the priest at a Sunday Mass being held in the country church of his small village. The boy, nervous in his new role at the altar, accidentally dropped the cruet of wine. The village priest immediately struck the boy sharply on the cheek, and in a very gruff voice, shouted so that many people could hear, "Leave the altar and don't come back!" That boy became Tito, the Communist leader who ruled Yugoslavia for many decades.

One day in a large city cathedral, a young boy was serving a bishop at a Sunday Mass. He, too, accidentally dropped the cruet of wine. The bishop turned to him, but rather than responding in anger, he gently whispered with a warm twinkle in his eyes, "Someday you will be a priest." That boy grew up to become Archbishop Fulton Sheen.

Words have power. The childhood phrase, "Sticks and stones can break my bones, but words can never hurt me," simply isn't true. Words do hurt. They wound—sometimes deeply.

Words also can reward, build self-esteem, create friendships, give hope, and render a blessing. Words can heal and drive us to achieve great things.

Watch what you say to a friend today! Are your words like poison to the heart, or do they drip with the sweetness of honey?

Reprove, rebuke, exhort, with
great patience and instruction.
2 TIMOTHY 4:2 NASB

The Tower of London has had many famous residents in its 900-year history, including Anne Boleyn, Thomas More, and Sir Walter Raleigh. These days, its most famous permanent residents are the colony of ravens that live within its walls. Though no one knows for sure when the first ravens took up residence at the Tower, great care is taken to assure that they remain there.

The seven ravens that currently reside at the Tower, are tended by the Ravenmaster, one of the Yeomen Warders who lives on the grounds and continues to guard the castle. The reason for all of this special attention is not that the ravens are so deeply loved by the British people. Ravens are actually rather antisocial birds. There's a legend, however, that if the ravens

> *Let each man think himself an act of God, his mind a thought of God, his life a breath of God.*

should desert the Tower of London, the kingdom of Britain will fall. Obviously, this legend is based on superstition, not fact. Nonetheless, all seven birds have their wings clipped on one side, rendering them flightless—just in case.[18]

Be honest. Is there anything you do to keep God on your side, "just in case"? Do you feel reading the Bible, praying, or giving money to the poor will keep God from deserting you; or do you really believe that God loves you for who you are, not what you do?

God created people in his own image;
God patterned them after himself.

GENESIS 1:27 NLT

Really great men and women are those who are natural, frank, and honest with everyone with whom they come into contact.

In ancient Greece, the philosopher Aristippus—considered by all who knew him to be the master of political craftiness—learned to get along well in royal circles by flattering the tyrant Denys. Not only did he flatter Denys, but he was proud that he did. In fact, Aristippus disdained less prosperous fellow philosophers and wise men who refused to stoop that low.

One day Aristippus saw his colleague Diogenes washing vegetables, and said to him, "If you would only learn to flatter King Denys, you would not have to be washing lentils." Diogenes looked up slowly and replied, "And you, if you had only learned to live on lentils, would not have to flatter King Denys."

Another way to regard flattery is this:

F—foolish

L—laughable

A—accolades

T—to

T—tell

E—everyone

R—'round

Y—you

Speak the truth sincerely. When the truth is painful, consider the option of remaining silent!

Don't show favoritism.

JAMES 2:1 NIV

Coach Gregory watched with pride as Rashaan Salaam accepted the Heisman Trophy. He recalled the hotshot eighteen-year-old who, finally free from his mother's tight discipline, had arrived in Colorado ready to devour the world. He said, "Rashaan was a gangster wannabe. He came here wearing all this red stuff, talking about gangs. He hadn't done it back home because his mother would never have tolerated it." Neither did Gregory. He never lectured or preached to Rashaan, but he did ask him questions.

'Tis better to be alone than in bad company.

When Rashaan came to him talking about his new friends, Gregory said, "Sure, they are your friends, but are you their friend? They know what you're trying to accomplish. They know the potential you have to do great things. If you are their friend, when they get ready to get into something, they'll say, 'Salaam, get out of here. Go home and study.'"

As a coach, Gregory wanted Salaam to "find daylight" and get into the end zone, but as his friend, he wanted him to live in the daylight and reach life's goal line as a productive citizen.

Winning a football game is never a one-man effort. It's a team effort. The same holds true for life, and the good news is you can choose the players on your team!

Do not be misled: "Bad company corrupts good character."

1 Corinthians 15:33 NIV

*The rotten apple spoils
his companion.*

Traffic laws are not designed so policemen can give tickets. They're written to help traffic run as safely and smoothly as possible. All it takes is one car driving the wrong direction on the wrong side of the highway to create havoc.

Consider Sweden's dilemma. Until 1965, drivers there drove on the left-hand side of the road. To conform to most of the rest of Europe's right-handed driving laws, Sweden decided it was time for a change. At 5:00 in the evening on a designated weekday, all drivers stopped their cars. Then, drivers moved their cars to the opposite side of the road. Obviously, it was a bit chaotic while the change occurred, but the government felt that a change at this hour would ensure that most drivers would be aware of what was happening. Pity the poor person working the swing shift!

It only takes one person going the wrong way to effect all of those near him going the right way. This happens not only on the road, but in life. The people you spend the most time with will influence your actions, as well as your opinions, for better or for worse. Which will it be? The company you keep will have an effect on the life you lead. Is there anyone you're spending time with who's leading you in a direction you know you shouldn't go?

He that walketh with wise men shall be wise: but a companion of fools shall be destroyed.
PROVERBS 13:20

We often think of great artists and musicians as having "bursts" of genius. More often, they are models of painstaking patience. Their greatest works tend to have been accomplished over long periods and in extreme hardships.

- Beethoven is said to have rewritten each bar of his music at least a dozen times.

- Josef Haydn produced more than eight hundred musical compositions before writing *The Creation*, the oratorio for which he is most famous.

Patience is bitter but its fruit is sweet.

- Michelangelo's *Last Judgment* is considered one of the twelve master paintings of the ages. It took him eight years to complete. He produced more than two thousand sketches and renderings in the process.

- Leonardo da Vinci worked on *The Last Supper* for ten years, often working so diligently that he would forget to eat.

When he was quite elderly, the pianist Ignace Paderewski was asked by an admirer, "Is it true that you still practice every day?" He replied, "Yes, at least six hours a day." The admirer said in awe, "You must have a world of patience." Paderewski said, "I have no more patience than the next fellow. I just use mine."

Put your patience to use in the pursuit of your dreams.

Ye have need of patience, that,
after ye have done the will of God,
ye might receive the promise.

HEBREWS 10:36

Some men dream of worthy accomplishments, while others stay awake and do them.

In 1972, *Life* magazine published a story about the amazing adventures of John Goddard. When he was fifteen, John's grandmother said, "If only I had done that when I was young." Determined not to have to make that statement at the end of his life, John wrote out 127 goals for his life.

He named ten rivers he wanted to explore and seventeen mountains he wanted to climb. He determined to become an Eagle Scout, a world traveler, and a pilot. Also on his list was: ride a horse in the Rose Bowl parade, dive in a submarine, retrace the travels of Marco Polo, read the Bible from cover to cover, and read the entire *Encyclopedia Britannica*.

He also planned to read the entire works of Shakespeare, Plato, Dickens, Socrates, Aristotle, and several other classic authors. He desired to learn to play the flute and violin, marry, have children (he had five), pursue a career in medicine, and serve as a missionary for his church.

Sound impossible? At the age of forty-seven, John Goddard had accomplished one hundred and three of his goals!

What goals have you set for your life? Write them down, memorize them, meditate on them, pursue them. Just dreaming will get you nowhere. Dreaming, setting goals, and actively working to accomplish those goals will make your dreams a reality.

Whatever you do, work at it with all your heart, as working for the Lord, not for men.
COLOSSIANS 3:23 NIV

William Penn, founding leader of the colony that became Pennsylvania, had these rules for conversation:

- "Avoid company where it is not profitable or necessary, and in those occasions, speak little, and last.

- Silence is wisdom where speaking is folly, and always safe.

- Some are so foolish as to interrupt and anticipate those that speak instead of hearing and thinking before they answer, which is uncivil, as well as silly.

The great test of a man's character is his tongue.

- If thou thinkest twice before thou speakest once, thou wilt speak twice the better for it.

- Better to say nothing than not to the purpose. And to speak pertinently, consider both what is fit and when it is fit to speak.

- In all debates, let truth be thy aim, not victory or an unjust interest; and endeavor to gain, rather than to expose, thy antagonist."

Though few achieve it, one of the greatest skills you can develop in life is the ability to control your tongue! It is an invaluable asset in every area of life; yet many people never appreciate its worth. How about you?

Self-control means controlling the tongue!
A quick retort can ruin everything.
PROVERBS 13:3 TLB

School seeks to get you ready for examinations; life gives the finals.

The Koh-in-noor diamond is among the world's most spectacular. It is part of the British crown jewels, presented to Queen Victoria by a maharajah in India when the maharajah was only a young boy.

Years later, when he was a grown man, the maharajah visited Queen Victoria in England. He asked that the stone be brought from the Tower of London, where it was kept in safety, to Buckingham Palace. The queen did as he requested.

Taking the diamond in his hand, he knelt before the queen and presented it back to her, saying, "Your Majesty, I gave this jewel when I was a child, too young to know what I was doing. I want to give it to you again in the fullness of my strength, with all of my heart and affection and gratitude, now and forever, fully realizing all that I do."

A day will come when you likely will look back and say, "I'm grateful for my teachers, and the lessons they taught me about discipline, concentration, hard work, cooperation, and the right and wrong ways to compete." Even more valuable will be the day when you look in a mirror and say, "Knowing what I now know about life, I see value in continuing to teach these lessons to myself."

Examine yourselves to see whether you are in the faith; test yourselves.
2 CORINTHIANS 13:5 NIV

The "Sixty-four Thousand-Dollar Question" was the hottest show on television in 1955. The more Joyce watched the program, the more she thought, "I could do that." At the time, Joyce had quit her teaching job to raise her daughter, and she and her husband were living on fifty dollars a month. She never dreamed of winning the top prize. Any prize at that point would have helped greatly.

Diligence is the mother of good fortune.

As a psychologist by training, Joyce analyzed the show. She saw that each contestant had a built-in incongruity—the marine who was a gourmet cook, the shoemaker who knew about opera. She looked at herself. She was a short, blond psychologist and mother, with no incongruity. After some thought, she decided to become an expert in boxing! She ate, drank, and slept boxing, studying its statistics, personalities, and history. When she felt she was ready, she applied as a contestant for the show, was accepted, won, and won again, until she eventually won the sixty-four thousand-dollar prize.

That experience led her to dream of a career as a television journalist who could translate the results of psychological research into terms that people could use in their everyday lives. Once she saw that possibility, there was no stopping Dr. Joyce Brothers.

True success never comes by chance. Diligently apply yourself to your goals, and your dreams will come true.

The plans of the diligent lead to profit.
PROVERBS 21:5 NIV

235

The road to success is dotted with many tempting parking places.

The first things to emerge at a baby giraffe's birth are its front hooves and head. Minutes later, the newborn is hurled from its mother's body, falling ten feet, and landing on its back. Within seconds, it rolls to an upright position with its legs tucked under its body. From this position, it views the world for the first time and shakes off any remaining birthing fluid.

The mother giraffe lowers her head just long enough to take a quick look at her calf, and then she does what seems to be a very unreasonable thing—she kicks her baby, sending it sprawling head over heels. If it doesn't get up, she kicks it again and again until the calf finally stands on its wobbly legs. Then what does the mother giraffe do? She kicks it off its feet! Why? She wants it to remember how to get up.

In the wild, baby giraffes must be able to get up as quickly as possible to stay with the herd and avoid becoming a meal for lions, hyenas, leopards, or wild dogs. The best way a mother giraffe has of ensuring her calf's safety is to teach it to get up quickly.

Don't complain if those who love you push you into action when you'd rather be in "park." They are doing you a favor.

Let us lay aside every weight, and the sin which doth so easily beset us, and let us run with patience the race that is set before us.
HEBREWS 12:1

On May 21, 1946, a scientist at Los Alamos was carrying out a necessary experiment in preparation for an atomic test to be conducted in the waters of the South Pacific. He had successfully performed this experiment many times before. It involved pushing two hemispheres of uranium together to determine the amount of U-235 needed for a chain reaction—the amount scientists call "a critical mass." Just as the mass became critical, he would push the hemispheres apart with his screwdriver, instantly stopping the chain reaction.

When you are laboring for others, let it be with the same zeal as if you were laboring for yourself.

That day, however, just as the material became critical, the screwdriver slipped. The hemispheres of uranium came too close together, and instantly, the room was filled with a dazzling bluish haze. Young Louis Soltin, instead of ducking and thereby possibly saving himself, tore the two hemispheres apart with his hands, thus interrupting the chain reaction.

In this instant, selfless act, he saved the lives of seven other people who were in the room. He, however, died nine days later.

Today, do something for someone else with the same energy you would use if you were doing it for yourself.

Each of you should look not only to your own interests, but also to the interests of others.

PHILIPPIANS 2:4 NIV

The Bible knows nothing of a hierarchy of labor. No work is degrading. If it ought to be done, then it is good work.

When David was twelve, he convinced a restaurant manager that he was actually sixteen and was hired as a lunch-counter waiter for twenty-five cents an hour. The place was owned by two Greek immigrant brothers, Frank and George, who had started their lives in America as a dishwasher and hot-dog seller.

David remembers that Frank and George set high standards and never asked anything of their employees that they wouldn't do themselves. Frank once told David, "As long as you try, you can always work for me." Trying meant everything from working hard to treating customers politely. Once, when Frank noticed a waitress giving a customer a rough time, he fired her on the spot and waited on the table himself. David determined that would never happen to him.

The usual tip for waiters in those days was a dime, but David discovered that if he brought the food out quickly and was especially polite, he sometimes got a quarter as a tip. He set a goal for himself to see how many customers he could wait on in one night. His record was one hundred!

Today, R. David Thomas is better known as "Dave," the founder and senior chairman of Wendy's International, Inc., a chain of forty-three hundred restaurants.

No matter what job you do, do it well.

To rejoice in his labour; this is the gift of God.
ECCLESIASTES 5:19

McCormick's father was what many might call a "tinkerer." A mechanical genius, he invented many farm devices. Sadly, however, he became the laughingstock of his community for attempting to make a grain-cutting device. For years, he worked on the project but never succeeded in getting it to operate reliably.

The ripest peach is highest on the tree.

In spite of the discouragement his father experienced and the continuing ridicule of neighbors, young McCormick took up the old machine as his own project. He also withstood years of experimentation and failure. Then one day, he succeeded in constructing a reaper that would harvest grain.

Even so, jealous opposition prevented the invention from being used for a number of years. McCormick was able to make sales only after he gave a personal guarantee to each purchaser that the reaper would do the job he claimed it could do. Finally, after decades of trial and error, hoping and waiting, a firm in Cincinnati agreed to manufacture 100 machines, and the famous McCormick reaper was born.

To get to the ripest peach on the highest branch, you need to climb one limb at a time and not be defeated by the scrape of bark, the occasional fall, and the frequent feeling of being left dangling!

Let us not become weary in doing good,
for at the proper time we will reap
a harvest if we do not give up.
GALATIANS 6:9 NIV

When you do the things you have to do when you have to do them, the day will come when you can do the things you want to do when you want to do them.

The bee is often described as busy. It deserves this adjective! To produce one pound of honey, a bee must visit fifty-six thousand clover heads. Since each head has sixty flower tubes, a bee must make a total of three million three hundred sixty thousand visits. In the process, the average bee would travel the equivalent of three times around the world.

To make just one *tablespoon* of honey, the amount that might go on a biscuit, a little bee must make forty-two hundred trips to the flowers, averaging about ten trips a day, each trip lasting approximately twenty minutes. It visits four hundred different flowers.

Day in, day out, the work of a bee is fairly unglamorous. It flies, it takes in nectar, it flies some more, and it deposits nectar. In the process, however, it produces and what it produces creates a place for it in the hive.

You may think your daily chores are a waste of time. Completing them is actually preparing you to succeed in life. One day you won't even have to think: *I must get disciplined. I must get to work. I must stick with it.* If you do your chores faithfully and to the best of your ability, the process will become a part of the way you tackle every challenge in life.

He becometh poor that dealeth with a slack hand: but the hand of the diligent maketh rich.

PROVERBS 10:4

Life is full of both irony and humor. Consider these little-known facts:

- In England, the Speaker of the House isn't allowed to speak.

- Winston Churchill was born in a ladies' room during a dance.

- Every year, more people are killed by donkeys than in plane crashes.

- The glue on Israeli postage stamps has to be certified kosher.

- An ostrich's eye is bigger than it's brain.

- In Paraguay, dueling is legal, as long as both participants are registered blood donors.

- The correct name for a pregnant goldfish is a "twit."

A man without mirth is like a wagon without springs, he is jolted disagreeably by every pebble in the road.

- Goethe swore he could only write if he had an apple rotting in his desk drawer.

- The man responsible for the voice of Bugs Bunny—Mel Blanc—was allergic to carrots.

- At Ben & Jerry's plant in Vermont, all of the waste from making ice cream is given to local pig farmers for use as feed. The pigs seem to love every flavor, except Mint Oreo.

It's true that life is hard; but it can also be beautiful, wondrous, and even downright silly. Being able to share a smile, or a laugh with someone will not only brighten their day, but yours as well. When you look at today, will you only see the "Mint Oreo" that you don't like, or all of the other great flavors from which you can choose?

A merry heart doeth good like a medicine: but a broken spirit drieth the bones.
PROVERBS 17:22

> *The truest self-respect is*
> *not to think of self.*

Leonard Bernstein was once asked which instrument was the most difficult to play. He thought for a moment and said, "The second fiddle. I can get plenty of first violinists, but to find someone who can play the second fiddle with enthusiasm—that's a problem. And if we have no second fiddle, we have no harmony."

General Robert E. Lee knew the value of playing second fiddle. This great general never stopped being a true southern gentleman. Once, while riding on a train to Richmond, he was seated at the rear of the car. All the other places were filled with officers and soldiers. A poorly dressed, elderly woman boarded the coach at a rural station, and finding no seat offered to her, she trudged down the aisle toward the back of the car.

Immediately, Lee stood up and offered her his seat. The other men then arose one after another and offered the general his seat. "No, gentlemen," he replied, "if there are no seats for this lady, there can be none for me!"

Selfishness is a sign of insecurity. Humility and the ability to consider the needs of others first are signs of self-respect.

Don't be selfish. . . . Be humble, thinking of others as better than yourself.

PHILIPPIANS 2:3 TLB

Doctors spend their lives trying help their patients, not harm them. In 1820, when a doctor from Putnam county discovered that his careless treatment of a six-week-old infant's eye infection had left her blind, he couldn't forgive himself. Trying to escape his sense of guilt and shame, he moved from his New York home.

If only he'd stayed long enough to get to know Fanny Crosby, the little girl whose life he'd changed. "If I could meet him now," Fanny wrote many year later, "I would say, 'Thank you, thank you' over and over again for making me blind."

Only he who can see the invisible can do the impossible.

Fanny believed that her blindness was a gift from God, because it helped her focus on writing the hymns that made her famous. During her ninety-four years, Fanny wrote more than 8,000 songs. Sometimes, she would have as many as forty different songs in various stages of composition in her head. Once she'd completed one, she'd dictate the song to a friend, who would then send it to her publisher. Fanny's positive attitude, incredible talent, and deep love of God, helped her do what many people would think impossible.[19]

There is much more to your life than what can be seen with human eyes. What have you done, with God's help, that you never could have done without Him?

By faith we understand that the entire universe was formed at God's command, that what we now see did not come from anything that can be seen.

HEBREWS 11:3 NLT

> *Always bear in mind that your own resolution to succeed is more important than any other one thing.*

Famous stage and film actress Helen Hayes believed her "resoluteness" about her own potential for success played an important role at the beginning of her career. She once told the story of a particular audition:

Before the authors gave me the script, they observed, in a matter-of-course manner, "Of course you play piano? You'll have to sing to your own accompaniment in the piece." As these alarming tidings were in the course of being made, I caught a bewildered look in my mother's eyes, and so I spoke up before she could. "Certainly I play piano," I answered.

As we left the theater, my mother sighed, "I hate to see you start under a handicap," she said. "What made you say you could play piano?" "The feeling that I will play before rehearsals begin," I said. We went at once to try to rent a piano and ended by buying one. I began lessons at once, practiced finger exercises till I could no longer see the notes—and began rehearsals with the ability to accompany myself. Since then, I have never lived too far from a piano.

What you believe about your own potential for success counts far more than what any other person may believe. Believe what God believes about you—you were created for success.

*The Lord G*OD *will help me; therefore shall I not be confounded: therefore have I set my face like a flint, and I know that I shall not be ashamed.*

ISAIAH 50:7

Many years ago in England, a small boy grew up speaking with a lisp. He was never a scholar in school. When war broke out involving his nation, he was rejected from service, and told "We need men." He once rose to address the House of Commons, and all present walked out of the room. In fact, he often spoke to empty chairs and echoes. One day, he became Prime Minister of Great Britain, and with stirring speeches and bold decisions, he led his nation to victory.

His name was Sir Winston Churchill.

Triumph is just "umph" added to try.

Many years ago in Illinois, a man with only a few years of formal education failed in business in '31, was defeated in a run for the state legislature in '32, again failed in business in '33, was elected to the legislature in '34, but defeated for speaker in '38. He was defeated for elector in '40, defeated for Congress in '43, elected to Congress in '46, but defeated in '48. He was defeated for Senate in '55, defeated for the vice-presidential nomination in '56, and defeated for the Senate in '58. But in 1860, he was elected president.

His name was Abraham Lincoln.

You cannot be defeated until you stop trying.

Whatsoever thy hand findeth to do,
do it with thy might.
ECCLESIASTES 9:10

Perseverance can do anything which genius can do, and a great many things which genius cannot.

As head of Marshall University's Journalism Department, W. Page Pitt earned a reputation as a no-nonsense professor with an expectation of excellence from his students. The standards he set for those in his classroom were no lower than the ones he set for his own life. Even though he lost 97 percent of his sight at the age of five, Pitt worked hard to be accepted into public school. He played baseball and football, relying on his sense of hearing to guide him where his sight could not. He diligently worked his way through college and graduate school to achieve his goal of becoming a journalism professor.

When asked by a student what he considered the greatest handicap anyone could face in life, Pitt replied, "Lethargy, irresponsibility, lack of ambition or desire: they are the real handicaps. If I do not teach you anything but to want to do something with your lives, this course will be a magnificent success!"[20]

Is there anything in your life that you consider a handicap? It may be physical, financial, situational, educational, relational, or even spiritual. Whatever you view as a "handicap" will inevitably become one. When you face adversity with courage, diligence, and a positive attitude, however, it becomes a challenge rather than a barrier that cannot be surmounted.

The thoughts of the diligent tend only to plenteousness.

PROVERBS 21:5

Henry P. Davison was a prominent American financier and one-time head of the American Red Cross. From poor beginnings, he worked his way up the ladder until he became the president of a large New York City bank.

While he was a cashier of that bank, a would-be robber came to his window, pointed a revolver at him, and passed a check across his window counter. The check was for one million dollars, payable to the Almighty. Davison remained calm, even though he realized the gravity of the situation. In a loud voice, he repeated the words on the check back to the person standing in front of him, emphasizing the "million dollars."

I think the one lesson I have learned is that there is no substitute for paying attention.

Then Davison graciously asked the would-be robber how he would like the million dollars for the Almighty. He then proceeded to count out small bills. In the meantime, the suspicion of a guard had been aroused by the strange request he had overheard. He disarmed the robber and prevented the theft.

In later years, Davison was known to advise those who asked, that courtesy, readiness, willingness, and alertness accomplish more for a person than simply being smart.

It has been said that one of the skills of a good communicator is the ability to listen. Paying attention to the words and actions of those around you may be the best schooling you'll ever receive.

We ought to give the more earnest heed to the things which we have heard, lest at any time we should let them slip.

HEBREWS 2:1

> *A good listener is not only*
> *popular everywhere, but after*
> *a while he knows something.*

Bloodhounds are known for their innate tracking abilities, due to their highly developed sense of smell. Even bloodhounds can get off track, though. If a herring is dragged across a trail that a bloodhound is following, the dog will become disoriented and lose the scent. The search will then come to a standstill.

In an argument, a "red herring" is something designed to throw a listener off track. Its intent is to divert another's attention from the main issue. When it comes to listening to the words of others, are there any "herrings" that cause you to lose track of where you should be going? Are you so intent on being heard that you're preparing what you're going to say next while others are speaking? Do you interrupt or finish what people are saying for them, because you think you know what they're going to say? Do you speak before you think? Can you listen to a conversation and not interject your own opinion? Do you feel what you have to say is more valuable than what others have to say?

Today, try an experiment. Really listen when others speak to you. Ask questions until you totally understand their point of view. Don't let your mind wander just because you're not speaking. Get rid of those smelly, old herrings. Who knows, you may in fact learn something new.

The ear that heareth the reproof
of life abideth among the wise.
PROVERBS 15:31

These words were spelled out in lights at the eighteenth Olympics in Tokyo: "The most important thing in the Olympic Games is not to win but to take part; just as the most important thing in life is not the triumph but the struggle. The essential thing is to have fought well."

The athletes who make it to the Olympic games are already the best of the best from each nation. Each athlete has excelled in ways few of his or her peers will ever reach; yet only one will wear a gold medal, one a silver, and one a bronze.

You may be disappointed if you fail, but you are doomed if you don't try.

Those who are so accustomed to winning face the devastating possibility of losing before not only their teammates, but also their countrymen; and in this age of worldwide television, before the entire world. How vital it is for these athletes to keep their perspective—that winning is not the important issue at the Olympics, but the opportunity to compete, to try, and to give one's best effort.

Regardless of the arena in which you compete, winning is not what is truly important. Trying and giving your best effort is what molds within you the lasting traits and character that are "better than gold."

The sluggard craves and gets nothing, but the desires of the diligent are fully satisfied.

PROVERBS 13:4 NIV

> *Success is never final;*
> *failure is never fatal;*
> *it is courage that counts.*

In *The Seven habits of Highly Effective People,* Stephen R. Covey writes:

One of the most inspiring times Sandra and I have ever had took place over a four-year period with a dear friend of ours named Carol, who had a wasting cancer disease. She had been one of Sandra's bridesmaids, and they had been best friends for more than twenty-five years.

When Carol was in the very last stages of the disease, Sandra spent time at her bedside helping her write her personal history. She returned from those protracted and difficult sessions almost transfixed by admiration for her friend's courage and her desire to write special messages to be given to her children at different stages in their lives.

Carol would take as little pain medication as possible, so that she would have full use of her mental and emotional faculties. Then she would whisper into a tape recorder or directly to Sandra. Carol was so proactive, so brave, and so concerned about others that she became an enormous source of inspiration to many people around her.

In today's world, courage is a desperately needed trait. Seek to develop it.

Be of good courage, and he shall strengthen your heart, all ye that hope in the LORD.
PSALM 31:24

Oswald Chambers is known as one of the greatest religious writers of all times. Even though Chambers' name is on thirty books, in actuality he authored only one, *Baffled to Fight Better.* The truth is that his wife, Gertrude, a court stenographer, took verbatim shorthand notes of her husband's sermons throughout the first seven years of their marriage. At the urging of friends, she prepared manuscripts from her notes that she then sent to be published.

When your work speaks for itself, don't interrupt.

Chambers most well-known title, *My Utmost for His Highest,* has been in print continuously since its publication in 1935. Partly as a result of his wife's tireless efforts, this book has become one of the top ten best-selling religious books of all time, with millions of copies in print. Gertrude didn't need recognition to assure her of a job well done. She realized that her gift was meant to be used behind the scenes.

Chambers once said, "Never make a principle out of your experience; let God be as original with other people as He is with you."[21]

What has God set before you to do? Don't compare yourself with those around you doing a similar job. You alone are uniquely designed to accomplish what God has created for you. Right now, what do you think that is? Is there anything you can do to improve the quality of that work?

Be sure to do what you should, for then you will enjoy the personal satisfaction of having done your work well, and you won't need to compare yourself to anyone else.

GALATIANS 6:4 NLT

> *Poor eyes limit your sight.*
> *Poor vision limits your deeds.*

One of the great disasters of history took place in 1271. In that year, Niccolo and Matteo Polo, the father and uncle of Marco Polo, visited Kubla Khan, who was considered the world ruler, with authority over all China, all India, and all of the East.

The Kubla Khan was attracted to the story of Christianity as Niccolo and Matteo told it to him. He said to them, "You shall go to your high priest and tell him on my behalf to send me a hundred men skilled in your religion, and I shall be baptized. And when I am baptized all my barons and great men will be baptized and their subjects will receive baptism, too. So there will be more Christians here than there are in your parts."

Nothing was done, however, in response to what the Kubla Khan had requested. After thirty years only a handful of missionaries were sent—too few too late.

The West apparently did not have the vision to see the East won to Christ. The mind boggles at the possible ways the world might be different today if thirteenth-century China, India, and the other areas of the Orient had been converted to Christianity.

If you lack vision today, ask God for it. He has wonders to reveal to you that you can't yet imagine!

Where there is no vision, the people perish.
PROVERBS 29:18

A fable is told of a young orphan boy who had no family and no one to love him. Feeling sad and lonely, he was walking through a meadow one day when he saw a small butterfly caught in a thorn bush. The more the butterfly struggled to free itself, the deeper the thorns cut into its fragile body. The boy carefully released the butterfly, but instead of flying away, the butterfly transformed into an angel right before his eyes.

People are lonely because they build walls instead of bridges.

The boy rubbed his eyes in disbelief as the angel said, "For your wonderful kindness, I will do whatever you would like." The little boy thought for a moment, and then said, "I want to be happy!" The angel replied, "Very well," and then leaned toward him, whispered in his ear, and vanished.

As the little boy grew up, there was no one in the land as happy as he. When people asked him the secret of his happiness, he would only smile and say, "I listened to an angel when I was a little boy."

On his deathbed, his neighbors rallied around him and asked him to divulge the key to his happiness. The old man finally told them: "The angel told me that everyone, no matter how secure they seemed, no matter how old or young, how rich or poor, had need of me."

You have something to give to everyone you come in contact with today. Build bridges instead of walls!

You should be like one big happy family . . . loving one another with tender hearts and humble minds.

1 PETER 3:8 TLB

271

> *Forgiveness means giving up your right to punish another.*

Kent and his wife awoke to the dull thud of eggs being thrown at the front of their house. This wasn't the first time. Chris, a former employee of Kent's, had taken offense at some of Kent's comments offered at his yearly review. Now, Chris seemed to be spending his weekends trying to get revenge. Between the prank phone calls, the toilet paper covered trees, and the dozens of eggs he'd cleaned off his car and front porch, Kent decided to take the matter into his own hands.

Instead of retaliating with his own carton of eggs, Kent invited Chris to lunch to discuss the matter. At first, Chris denied doing anything, so Kent changed his approach. He asked Chris if there was anything he needed to say that he felt Kent had not listened to before. Chris then began opening up, expressing his anger over Kent's criticism of his work. After confronting Kent with what he was feeling, however, some of that anger began to disappear. From that day on, the weekend pranks disappeared as well.

Your approach to a matter can mean the difference between a peaceful relationship or a hostile one. Is there any situation in your life you need to approach in a different manner? If so, what is one step you can take today toward remedying the problem?

"When you stand praying, if you hold anything against anyone, forgive him, so that your Father in heaven may forgive you your sins."

MARK 11:25 NIV

Growing to the height of the Statue of Liberty and the circumference of a Greyhound bus, redwood trees are the largest living things on this planet. A typical grove of redwood trees has the densest biomass (that is the amount of living matter in a designated area) of any place on earth, including the Amazonian rainforest. Their bark, which can grow up to a foot thick, is resistant to fire, drought, and termites. Surviving for hundreds of years, these giants of the plant world exist in only three places—the northern coast of California, a small area of the Sierra Nevada mountain range, and a remote valley in China.

Unity creates strength.

Considering their massive height and weight, most people would assume that redwoods have an extraordinarily deep root system. Actually, their roots are fairly shallow. Redwoods instead draw their needed strength to stand firm by growing together in groves. In so doing, their shallow roots are interconnected with the roots of their neighboring redwoods. This enables the entire grove to better withstand the elements.

When you need strength to stand firm in your convictions, with whom are you interconnected? Who do you lean on when the storms of life blow your way? Having family, friends, and mentors you can turn to for support will help you stand tall, no matter the circumstance.

Always keep yourselves united in the Holy Spirit, and bind yourselves together with peace.
EPHESIANS 4:3 NLT

> *Abilities are like tax deductions—*
> *we use them or we lose them.*

Andrew Carnegie, considered to be one of the first to emphasize self-esteem and the potential for inner greatness, was famous for his ability to produce millionaires from among his employees. One day a reporter asked him, "How do you account for the fact you have forty-three millionaires working for you?"

Carnegie replied, "They weren't rich when they came. We work with people the same way you mine gold. You have to remove a lot of dirt before you find a small amount of gold."

Andrew Carnegie knew how to bring about change in people. He helped them realize their hidden treasure within, inspired them to develop it, and then watched with encouragement as their lives were transformed.

The philosopher and psychologist William James once said, "Compared to what we ought to be, we are only half awake. We are making use of only a small part of our physical and mental resources. Stating the thing broadly, the human individual thus lives far within his limits. He possesses powers of various sorts which he habitually fails to use."

In other words, most people only develop a fraction of their abilities. Go for a bigger percentage in your life. Find the gold within!

God has given gifts to each of you from his great variety of spiritual gifts. Manage them well so that God's generosity can flow through you.
1 PETER 4:10 NLT

Several years ago, a well-known television circus developed an act involving Bengal tigers. The act was performed live before a large audience. One night, the tiger trainer went into the cage with several tigers, and the door was routinely locked behind him. Spotlights flooded the cage, and television cameras moved in close so the audience could see every detail as he skillfully put the tigers through their paces.

Courage is resistance to fear, mastery of fear—not absence of fear.

In the middle of the performance, the worst happened: the lights went out. For nearly thirty long seconds, the trainer was locked in with the tigers in the darkness. With their superb night vision, the tigers could see him, but he could not see them. Still, he survived. When the lights came back on, he calmly finished his performance.

When the trainer was asked how he felt, he admitted to feeling chilling fear at first, but then, he said he realized that even though he couldn't see the big cats, they didn't know he couldn't see them. "I just kept cracking my whip and talking to them until the lights came on," he said. "They never knew I couldn't see them as well as they could see me."

Keep talking back to the tigers of fear that seem to be stalking you.

Yea, though I walk through the valley of the shadow of death, I will fear no evil: for thou art with me; thy rod and thy staff they comfort me.

PSALM 23:4

*Prayer is an invisible tool
that is wielded in a visible world.*

Both a major thoroughfare in Tel Aviv and a bridge that spans the Jordan River are named in honor of Viscount Edmund Henry Hynman Allenby, a British soldier. As commander of the Egyptian Expeditionary Forces, he outwitted and defeated the Turks in Palestine in 1917 and 1918, conquering Jerusalem without ever firing a single gun.

As a British soldier, Allenby was noncommittal about the official British policies concerning the establishment of a Jewish national home, but he did have a deep understanding of the Jews' desire to dwell in Palestine. At a reception in London, he spoke of being a little boy kneeling to say his evening prayers and repeating with his childhood lisp the words his mother prayed: "And, O Lord, we would not forget Thine ancient people, Israel; hasten the day when Israel shall again be Thy people and shall be restored to Thy favor and to their land."

Allenby concluded, "I never knew then that God would give me the privilege of helping to answer my own childhood prayers."

What you pray today may well be part of tomorrow's work. The world you envision in prayer may well be the world in which you one day will live!

The weapons of our warfare are not carnal, but mighty through God to the pulling down of strong holds.

2 CORINTHIANS 10:4

A strange memorial can be found in the Mount Hope Cemetery of Hiawatha, Kansas. John M. Davis, an orphan, developed a strong dislike for his wife's family and insisted that none of his fortune go to them. He also refused requests that he eventually bequeath his estate for a hospital desperately needed in the area.

Money is like an arm or leg: use it or lose it.

Instead, after his wife died in 1930, Mr. Davis chose to invest in an elaborate tomb for himself and his wife. The tomb includes a number of statues depicting the couple at various stages of their lives. One statue is of Mr. Davis as a lonely man seated beside an empty chair. It is titled "the vacant chair." Another shows him placing a wreath in front of his wife's tombstone. Many of the statues are made of Kansas granite. No money was left for the memorial's upkeep.

Today, largely because of its weight, this costly memorial is slowly sinking into the ground. It has become weathered and worn from the strong winds in this plains state. The townspeople regard the Davis tomb as an "old man's folly," and many predict that within the next fifty years, the memorial will have become obliterated beyond recognition and will need to be demolished. What could have been a living legacy will eventually become granite dust.

The Bible encourages us many times not to hoard up money to be used for our own selfish desires, but to be kind to the poor. When we do so, God blesses us with more. The more we give, the more we receive, and our legacy will last well into the future instead of sinking into oblivion.

"Sell your possessions and give to the poor. Provide purses for yourselves that will not wear out, a treasure in heaven that will not be exhausted, where no thief comes near and no moth destroys."

LUKE 12:33 NIV

*In trying times,
don't quit trying.*

In 1894, a sixteen-year-old boy found this note from his rhetoric teacher at Harrow, in England, attached to his report card: "A conspicuous lack of success." The young man kept on trying and went on to become one of the most famous speakers of the twentieth century. His name was Winston Churchill.

In 1902, an aspiring twenty-eight-year-old writer received a rejection letter from the poetry editor of *The Atlantic Monthly*. Returned, with a batch of poems he had sent, was this curt note: "Our magazine has no room for your vigorous verse." He kept on trying, however, and went on to see his work published. The poet's name was Robert Frost.

In 1905, the University of Bern turned down a Ph.D. dissertation as being fanciful and irrelevant. The young physics student who wrote the dissertation kept on trying and went on to develop some of his ideas into widely accepted theories. His name was Albert Einstein.

When rejection shakes your resolve and dims your goals, keep on trying. If you do not quit, one day, you will be living out your dreams!

*The righteous also shall hold on
his way, and he that hath clean
hands shall be stronger and stronger.*
JOB 17:9

After years of hard work and financial sacrifice, the Clark family was finally ready to set out on the adventure of a lifetime. Getting passports and tickets to travel from Scotland to the United States was no small task for a family with seven children. The promise of a new life in America, though, was all the incentive they needed.

A week before their departure, the Clark's youngest son was bitten by a dog. With the possibility of the boy getting rabies, the doctor hung a yellow sheet on the Clark's front door. This let everyone know the house was under quarantine for fourteen days. Anger and disappointment filled every heart in the Clark household, but nothing could be done. The oceanliner left without them.

> *Let us not say,
> "Every man is the
> architect of his
> own fortune;"
> but let us say,
> "Every man is
> the architect of his
> own character."*

Five days later, all of Scotland had heard the news. The unsinkable Titanic had sunk. Were it not for a random dog bite, the Clarks could have lost their lives along with the hundreds of others who drowned that night in the frigid sea.

Every life is a story, written by an unseen Hand. You have no control over when you're born or when you'll die, but one thing is always in *your* hands—the character of the role you'll play. Who will you be? A man of integrity? A woman deserving of honor? The choice is up to you.

Till I die I will not remove mine integrity from me. My righteousness I hold fast, and will not let it go: my heart shall not reproach me so long as I live.

JOB 27:5-6

It is impossible for that man to despair who remembers that his Helper is omnipotent.

E. Stanley Jones tells the story of a missionary who became lost in an African jungle. Looking around, he saw nothing but bush and a few clearings. He stumbled about until he finally came across a native hut. He asked one of the natives if he could lead him out of the jungle and back to the mission station. The native agreed to help him.

"Thank you!" exclaimed the missionary. "Which way do I go?" The native replied, "Walk." And so they did, hacking their way through the unmarked jungle for more than an hour.

In pausing to rest, the missionary looked around and had the same overwhelming sense that he was lost. Again, all he could see was bush and a few clearings. "Are you quite sure this is the way?" he asked. "I don't see any path."

The native looked at him and replied, "Bwana, in this place there is no path. I am the path."

When we have no clues about which direction we're going, we must remember that God, who guides us, is omniscient—all-wise. When we feel alone, we must remember that God is omnipresent—always with us. When we are weak, we must remember that God is omnipotent—all-powerful. He is everything we need.

I will lift up my eyes to the mountains;
From whence shall my help come?
My help comes from the LORD,
Who made heaven and earth.
PSALM 121:1-2 NASB

In the 1960s, in the tuberculosis ward of a hospital in India, Doug Nichols was just another patient. He'd traveled as a missionary from America to help others, but here he was needing help himself. Although weak and suffering from frequent coughing spells, Doug tried to share his love of God with those around him. None of the other patients seemed interested in what he had to say.

One morning, Doug noticed an elderly man trying to get out of bed, with no success. A little later, a nurse approached the old man and exploded in anger. She slapped the man for soiling his bed. Weak and embarrassed, the old man began to cry. About 2:00 in the morning, the scene began to repeat itself. The old man tried to get out of bed but

Service is nothing but love in work clothes.

fell back, exhausted. This time, Doug got out of his own bed and tenderly carried the frail man to the rest room.

Later that morning, Doug awoke to the scent of hot tea being served to him by another patient. That patient, along with doctors, nurses, and many other patients in the hospital, all wanted to hear about the God Doug had tried to tell them about earlier.[22]

Doug's simple act of caring meant more than a sermon ever could have. What kind of message do your actions speak to those around you?

"The more lowly your service to others, the greater you are. To be the greatest, be a servant."

MATTHEW 23:11 TLB

Those that have done nothing in life are not qualified to judge those that have done little.

In the 1700s, an English cobbler kept a map of the world on his workshop wall so that he might be reminded to pray for the nations of the world. As the result of such prayer, he became especially burdened for a specific missionary outreach. He shared this burden at a meeting of ministers, but was told by a senior minister, "Young man, sit down. When God wants to convert the heathen, He will do it without your help or mine."

The cobbler, William Carey, did not let this man's remarks put out the flame of his concern. When he couldn't find others to support the missionary cause that had burdened his soul, he became a missionary himself. His pioneering efforts in India are legendary, and his mighty exploits for God are recorded by many church historians.

Be careful how you respond to the enthusiasm of others. Don't dampen someone's zeal for God. Be cautious in how you respond to the new ideas of another, that you don't squelch their God-given creativity.

Be generous and kind in evaluating the work of others so that you might encourage those things which are worthy. Be slow to judge and quick to praise. Then pray for the same in your own life!

Judge not, and ye shall not be judged:
condemn not, and ye shall not be condemned.
LUKE 6:37

A young man once came to Jesus asking Him what he needed to do to have eternal life. Jesus replied that he should keep the commandments. The young man then claimed that he had always kept them. Jesus advised, *If you want to be perfect, go, sell your possessions and give to the poor. . . . Then come, follow me* (Matthew 19:21 NIV).

People, places, and things were never meant to give us life. God alone is the author of a fulfilling life.

The Scriptures tell us that the young man *went away sad, because he had great possessions* (vs. 22). The young man not only had great possessions, but apparently those possessions had him! He couldn't bear to part with earthly, temporary goods in order to obtain heavenly, eternal goods. Jesus also taught, of course, that heaven's "wealth" can be ours now.

This young man didn't have to wait until he died to receive the benefits of eternal life. If he had been willing to give up his hold on his "stuff," he could have enjoyed great joy, peace, and fulfillment in life—things he was apparently lacking, or he wouldn't have asked Jesus that particular question.

Take a look at your possessions today. Find those things you can give away to someone in need. Discover how rewarding giving can be!

I am come that they might have life, and that they might have it more abundantly.
JOHN 10:10

*One man with courage
makes a majority.*

An ancient Greek legend is told of two loyal friends, Damon and Pythias. They lived in Syracuse during the reign of Dionysius I, a notoriously tyrannical ruler. When Pythias was condemned to death for plotting against Dionysius I, he begged to be released long enough to return to his home and get his affairs in order. Damon rose to his defense, putting his own life up as a security that Pythias would return to receive his sentence.

As the date of the execution drew near, Pythias' return was delayed. Damon was ridiculed for his foolhardiness and misplaced trust. After all, a condemned man who was given a taste of freedom would most likely never return. Damon continued to believe his friend would be true to his word. On the day that Damon was being prepared for execution, Pythias did return, just as he promised he would. Dionysius I was so impressed with the friends' loyalty that he not only let them both live, but asked that they include him in their bond of friendship, teaching him how to be the kind of friend that they had been to one another.[23]

God's loyalty to you is even stronger than Damon's was to Pythias. God is on your side, even when it seems the rest of the world isn't.

Be strong and of a good courage . . .
for the LORD thy God . . . will
not fail thee, nor forsake thee.
DEUTERONOMY 31:6

When Ruth Bell was a teenager, she was sent from her childhood home in China to school in Korea. At the time, she fully intended to follow in her parents' footsteps and become a missionary. She envisioned herself a confirmed "old maid," ministering to the people of Tibet. While at school, however, Ruth did give some serious thought to the kind of husband that she *might* consider. As she tells in her book *A Time for Remembering,* she listed these particulars:

You will never make a more important decision than the person you marry.

If I marry: He must be so tall that when he is on his knees, as one has said, he reaches all the way to heaven. His shoulders must be broad enough to bear the burden of a family. His lips must be strong enough to smile, firm enough to say no, and tender enough to kiss. Love must be so deep that it takes its stand in Christ and so wide that it takes the whole lost world in. He must be active enough to save souls. He must be big enough to be gentle and great enough to be thoughtful. His arms must be strong enough to carry a little child.

Ruth Bell never did become a full-time missionary in Tibet. She did, however, find a man worth marrying—Billy Graham. As his wife, Ruth Bell Graham became a missionary to the whole world!

It's crucial to marry the right person. Think about the qualities that you would like to have in a mate. If you haven't already, begin to pray now that God will prepare the heart of the one He intends for you to marry.

Therefore shall a man leave his father and his mother, and shall cleave unto his wife: and they shall be one flesh.

GENESIS 2:24

> *The Bible has a word*
> *to describe "safe" sex:*
> *it's called marriage.*

The 1960s were known for many rebellions, among them the sexual revolution. "Free love" spilled from the hippie movement into the mainstream American culture. Premarital sexual relations sanctioned by the "new morality" became openly flaunted.

One of the unexpected results of this trend, however, received little publicity. As reported by Dr. Francis Braceland, past president of the American Psychiatric Association and editor of the *American Journal of Psychiatry,* an increasing number of young people were admitted to mental hospitals during that time. In discussing this finding at a National Methodist Convocation of medicine and Theology, Braceland concluded, "A more lenient attitude on campus about premarital sexual experience has imposed stresses on some college women severe enough to cause emotional breakdown."

Looking back over the years since the "new morality" was sanctioned by a high percentage of the American culture, one finds a rising number of rapes, abortions, divorces, premarital pregnancies, single-family homes, and cases of sexually transmitted diseases, including herpes and HIV.

The evidence is compelling: the old morality produced safer, healthier, and happier people!

Marriage should be honored by all, and the marriage bed kept pure, for God will judge the adulterer and all the sexually immoral.

HEBREWS 13:4 NIV

When Gina's "to do" list spilled over onto a second sheet of paper, she knew the day was going to be a wild one. There wasn't a moment to spare. When Gina entered the freeway, it looked more like a parking lot. So much for her best laid plans.

In the distance, she saw an elderly woman standing on the side of the freeway. As traffic inched forward, Gina saw steam rising from under the hood of the woman's car. *Surely, someone will stop to help,* Gina thought. She reviewed her own jam-packed schedule in her mind, but the lost look on the woman's face prompted Gina to pull over.

Nothing valuable can be lost by taking time.

After a few friendly words of introduction, Gina used her cell phone to contact a tow truck. With profuse thanks, the woman insisted Gina go on about her business, reassuring her that she'd be fine waiting for the mechanic by herself. As Gina pulled back onto the freeway, she noticed the traffic was moving again. Back to her "to do" list.

That afternoon at work, a bouquet of flowers were delivered to Gina's desk. The card read, "Thanks again from your freeway friend, Dot." Making a friend, or being one, requires time, but the time you spend reaching out to someone else is never wasted. How flexible are you when it comes to helping someone in need?

Just as you want men to treat you,
treat them in the same way.
Luke 6:31 NASB

Say "thank you" when you receive a favor, and "excuse me" or "pardon me" when needing to interrupt a discussion.

Which virtuous behaviors on earth will still be required in Heaven?

- Courage? No. There will be nothing to fear in Heaven.

- Hope? No. We will have all that we desire.

- Faith? No. We will be in the presence of the Source of our faith, and all those things for which we have believed will have their fulfillment in Him and by His hand.

- Acts of charity toward those in need? No. There will be no hunger, thirst, nakedness, or homelessness in Heaven. All needs will be supplied.

- Sympathy? No, for there will be no more tears and no more pain.

- Courtesy? Yes! There will still be room for the exercise of courtesy—the kind greeting, the simple manners that offend no one, but ease the way of all.

Good manners are important. They put people at ease, which in turn makes them more cooperative and happy.

Immanuel Kant once said, "Always treat a human being as a person, that is, as an end in himself, and not merely as a means to your end." Strive to impart dignity and self-worth to all you meet. Consider it dress rehearsal for your future life in Heaven!

While we have opportunity,
let us do good to all men.
GALATIANS 6:10 NASB

A mother watched with raised eyebrows as her two sons took a hammer and a few nails from the kitchen utility drawer and scurried to one of the boys' rooms, giggling and talking in low voices. When she didn't hear any hammering, she continued with her chores. Then from the kitchen window, she saw one of the boys take a stepladder from the garage. He disappeared from sight before she could call to him. A few minutes later her other son came into the kitchen to ask if she had any rope.

Knock and ask permission before entering someone's room.

"No, what's going on?" Mom said. Her son said, "Nothin.'" Mom pressed, "Are you sure?" but her son was out of sight.

Suspicious, Mom went to her son's room and found the door closed and locked. She knocked.

"What are you boys doing in there?" she asked. One son replied, "Nothin.'"

Suspecting great mischief, she demanded entrance. "I want you to open this door right now!" she said. A few seconds later, the door popped open, and her son shouted, "Surprise!" as he handed her a rather crudely wrapped present. "Happy birthday, Mom!" the other boy added. Truly surprised, the mother stammered, "But what about the hammer, nails, ladder, and rope?" The boys grinned, "Oh Mom, those were just decoys."

Show respect for everyone.
1 PETER 2:17 NLT

Yield to those in authority.

While driving down a country road, a man came to a very narrow bridge. In front of the bridge, there was a sign that read, "Yield." Seeing no oncoming cars, the man continued across the bridge to his destination. On his way back, the man came to the same one-lane bridge, now from the opposite direction. To his surprise, he saw another "Yield" sign posted there.

Curious, he thought, *I'm sure there was one positioned on the other side.* Sure enough, when he reached the other side of the bridge and looked back, he saw the sign. Yield signs had been placed at both ends of the bridge, obviously with the intent that drivers from both directions were requested to give each other the right-of-way. It was a reasonable and doubly sure way to prevent a head-on collision.

If you find yourself in a combative situation with someone in authority, it is always wise to yield to them. If they have authority over you, a lack of respect will put you in a position to be punished or reprimanded. If you are of equal authority, an exercise of your power will only build resentment in a person better kept as an ally.

Pray this way for kings and all others who are in authority, so that we can live in peace and quietness, in godliness and dignity.

1 TIMOTHY 2:2 NLT

The letters RSVP stand for the French phrase *responde s'il vous plait,* which means "please respond." This phrase on an invitation asks that you let the host know whether or not you plan to attend the function.

Occasionally, a hand-written invitation will say, "RSVP, regrets only." In this case, you are expected to notify the host only if you will *not* be attending. A truly thoughtful guest, however, who plans to attend will still call or mail a note to the host to say thank you for the invitation and confirm that he will be attending.

> *RSVP promptly when you receive an invitation.*

Imagine that you planned a catered party for fifty guests and you were paying twenty-five dollars per guest. Then imagine that half your guests failed to respond, and ten of them did not show up. You would be spending two hundred and fifty dollars for people who simply were not considerate enough to let you know they would not be present. Would you consider those people to be thoughtful friends?

Be the kind of guest that you would like to have attend your own fanciest party!

Make the most of every opportunity
for doing good.
EPHESIANS 5:16 NLT

Return what you borrow,
on time and in good condition.

A store once had the following lay-away policy: "We hold it in the store while you pay for it. You're mad. You take it from the store, and you don't pay for it. We're mad. Better that you're mad."

Mark Twain's neighbor may have had this policy in mind when Twain asked to borrow a certain book he had spotted in his neighbor's library. "Why, yes, Mr. Clemens, you're more than welcome to it," the neighbor said. "But I must ask you to read it here. You know I make it a rule never to let any book go out of my library."

Several days later, the neighbor came to Twain's house and asked if he could borrow his lawn mower since his had been taken to the repair shop. "Why, certainly," the humorist replied. "You're more than welcome to it. But I must ask you to use it only in my yard. You know I make it a rule."

Treat what you borrow as if it were a prized possession, returning it promptly. If something happens to it while it is in your possession, make repairs or replace it, not to your satisfaction, but to the satisfaction of the owner. Always remember, even though the item is in your hands, it is not yours. It still belongs to the other person.

Don't act thoughtlessly, but try to understand what the Lord wants you to do.
EPHESIANS 5:17 NLT

Mr. Brown was in his final year of seminary, preparing to become a pastor. The policy of his school called for him to be available at a moment's notice to fill in for local churches that might need a preacher. Mr. Brown eagerly awaited such an opportunity, and at long last, his moment arrived. The pastor of a country church was called away on an emergency, and Mr. Brown was asked to fill the pulpit.

Having waited so long for the opportunity, and having so much to say, Mr. Brown soon became completely immersed in his own words. The more he preached, the more he became inspired to preach. When he glanced at his watch, he was shocked to see that he had preached for a full hour. He was truly embarrassed since he had

> *Be on time for appointments; leave on time, too, for nothing is more boring than someone who overstays his welcome.*

been allotted only thirty minutes to preach. Knowing that he had preached well into the lunch hour, he made a heartfelt apology to the congregation and sat down.

A young woman hurried to him after the service ended. Obviously more impressed with his personality and appearance—and perhaps his availability—than she was with his message, she gushed, "Oh, Brother Brown, you needn't have apologized. You really didn't talk long—it just seemed long."

The old rule of thumb is, "Always leave them wanting more."

Don't think only about your own affairs, but be interested in others, too, and what they are doing.

PHILIPPIANS 2:4 NLT

*When you were born, you cried
and the world rejoiced. Live your
life in such a manner that when you
die the world cries and you rejoice.*

Ellicott is a far cry from Broadway. This tiny farming town of 6,100 people lies on the eastern plains of Colorado. Thanks to Pat Thisted, however, Ellicott High School students brought productions such as *Hamlet* and *Henry IV*, complete with broomstick swords, to this tight-knit community. For more than twenty years, Pat taught drama and English. Her expertise and dedication to making a difference in the lives of high school students has made a big impact on the small town.

On May 28, 2001, a tornado ripped through Ellicott. Seventeen people were injured as the roaring winds toppled mobile homes and destroyed Ellicott High. Local reporters commented on how lucky the community was to have so few injuries. One of the reasons for this "luck" was that many of Ellicott's residents were in nearby Colorado Springs. They were there to attend a "visitation" for Pat Thisted. Her funeral was scheduled for the following day.

After her year-long battle with cancer, Pat had insisted there be no flowers at her funeral. Instead, she requested donations be made to a memorial fund benefiting Ellicott High. She had no idea how desperately that fund would be needed to rebuild the school where she'd served for so long.[24] Even in death, Pat Thisted was a blessing to others. What kind of legacy would you like to leave on this world?

The memory of the righteous will be a blessing.

PROVERBS 10:7 NIV

Endnotes

1. (p. 13) Dr. Harold Sala, *Heroes: People Who Made a Difference in Our World* (Uhrichsville, Ohio: Promise Press, 1998) p. 234.

2. (p. 21) Nat G. Bodian, *The Joy of Publishing* (Fairfield, Iowa: Open Horizons Publishing Company, 1996) pp. 49-51.

3. (p. 27) *Jokes and Anecdotes,* edited by Joe Claro (New York: Random House, 1996) p. 163.

4. (p. 39) Dr. Harold Sala, *Heroes: People Who Made a Difference in Our World* (Uhrichsville, Ohio: Promise Press, 1998) pp. 180-181.

5. (p. 45) Rewrite of Internet story from *goodstories.com,* attributed to *The Church Humor Digest* (Memphis: Castle Books).

6. (p. 49) David K. Fremon, *The Holocaust Heroes* (Springfield, New Jersey: Enslow Publishers, Inc., 1998) pp. 58-64.

7. (p. 51) Nat G. Bodian, *The Joy of Publishing* (Fairfield, Iowa: Open Horizons Publishing Company, 1996) p. 124.

8. (p. 67) Dr. Harold Sala, *Heroes: People Who Made a Difference in Our World* (Uhrichsville, Ohio: Promise Press, 1998) pp. 59-61.

9. (p. 105) Ibid., pp. 277-78.

10. (p. 109) Warren W. Wiersbe, *Victorious Christians You Should Know* (Grand Rapids, Michigan: Baker Books, 1997) pp. 102-108.

11. (p. 123) Dr. Harold Sala, *Heroes: People Who Made a Difference in Our World* (Uhrichsville, Ohio: Promise Press, 1998) pp. 225-226.

12. (p. 147) Pam Brown, *Father Damien* (Milwaukee: Gareth Stevens Publishing, 1988.)

13. (p. 157) *The Dictionary of Cultural Literacy* (Boston, Massachusetts: Houghton Mifflin Company, 1993) p. 160.

14. (p. 165) Warren W. Wiersbe, *Victorious Christians You Should Know* (Grand Rapids, Michigan: Baker Books, 1997) pp. 74-80.

15. (p. 181) *Reader's Digest* (May, 1994) p. 114.

16. (p. 189) Dr. Harold Sala, *Heroes: People Who Made a Difference in Our World* (Uhrichsville, Ohio: Promise Press, 1998) pp. 201-202, 265-266.

17. (p 209) Ibid., p. 265.

18. (p. 218) Michael Leapman, *Eyewitness Travel Guides* (London, New York, New York: DK Publishing, Inc., 2000) p.154.

19. (p. 251) Warren W. Wiersbe, *Victorious Christians You Should Know* (Grand Rapids, Michigan: Baker Books, 1997) pp. 22-26.

20. (p. 257) Dr. Harold Sala, *Heroes: People Who Made a Difference in Our World* (Uhrichsville, Ohio: Promise Press, 1998) pp. 125-126.

21. (p. 267) Warren W. Wiersbe, *Victorious Christians You Should Know* (Grand Rapids, Michigan: Baker Books, 1997) pp. 53-59.

22. (p. 291) Dr. Harold Sala, *Heroes: People Who Made a Difference in Our World* (Uhrichsville, Ohio: Promise Press, 1998) pp. 29-31.

23. (p. 297) *The Dictionary of Cultural Literacy* (Boston, Massachusetts: Houghton Mifflin Company, 1993) p. 33.

24. (p. 317) *The Gazette* Colorado Springs: Colorado, (May 29, 2001).

Acknowledgments

We acknowledge and thank the following people for the quotes used in this book: Abraham Lincoln (10, 252), Les Brown (12), H. E. Jansen (14), John D. Rockefeller Jr. (16), Comte Georges-Louis Leclerc De Buffon (20), Harry Emerson Fosdick (22, 204), Ralph Waldo Emerson (24, 40), Daniel Webster (26), Charles Haddon Spurgeon (28, 108, 134), Phaedrus (32), Syrus (38, 200), Chuck Swindoll (44), Frank Borman (46), Ralph Washington Sockman (48), Josiah Gilbert Holland (50), Martha Washington (52), Sister Corita (54), Calvin Coolidge (56, 210), Sprat (62), Dr. Eugene Swearinger (64, 68), Thomas Jefferson (66, 126), Robert C. Edward (70), Andrew Jackson (72), Ed Cole (74, 86, 280), Woodrow Wilson (80, 132), John A. Shedd (82), Pablo Casals (88), Roy Disney (96), Helen Keller (98), Seneca (100), Aristotle (102, 162), Dwight L. Moody (104), William A. Ward (106), Moliere (110), Bob Bales (112), Charles C. Noble (114), Samuel Johnson (116, 292), Eleanor Roosevelt (118), John Skulley (120), George Bernard Shaw (122), Oprah Winfrey (124), Benjamin Franklin (130, 224), Terence (138), Henry Wadsworth Longfellow (144), Josh Billings (148), Jean Paul Richter (152), William James (154), Samuel Butler (156), H. P. Liddon (158), George Elliott (160), John R. Rice (164), William H. Danforth (166, 186, 220), Thomas Edison (168), Dwight Moody (170), George Edward Woodberry (172), Ronald E. Osborn (174), Bill Cosby (176), Winston Churchill (178, 264), Thomas Carlyle (182), Bacon (184), Lillian Dickson (188), Denis Diderot (190), Earl Nightingale (192), Horace (194), Louis D. Brandeis (196), Hannah More (198), Orlando A. Bri (202), Victor Hugo (206), David Dunn (208), Mark Twain (212, 278), Roy L. Smith (214), George Herbert (216), Philip James Bailey (218), George Washington (222), Oswald Chambers (230), Say (232), Cervantes (234), Ben Patterson (240), James Whitcomb Riley (242), Zig Ziglar (244), Henry Ward Beecher (246, 248, 256), Frank Gaines (250), Diane Sawyer (258), Wilson Mizner (260), Beverly Sills (262), Henry J. Kaiser (266), Franklin Field (268), Joseph Newton (270), Dennis Rainey (272), Henry Ford (282), George Dana Boardman (286), Jeremy Taylor (288), Gary Smalley and John Trent (294, 300), Dr. Eugene Swearingen (298).

Additional copies of this book and other titles
in the *God's Little Devotional Book* series
are available from your local bookstore.

God's Little Devotional Book
God's Little Devotional Book for Students
God's Little Devotional Book for Dads
God's Little Devotional Book for Moms
God's Little Devotional Book for Women
God's Little Devotional Book for Men
God's Little Devotional Book for Couples
God's Little Devotional Book for Teens

If you have enjoyed this book, or if it has impacted
your life, we would like to hear from you.

Please contact us at:

Honor Books
Department E
P.O. Box 55388
Tulsa, Oklahoma 74155

Or by e-mail at info@honorbooks.com

Honor Books
Tulsa, Oklahoma